Valuing and Educating
Young People

of related interest

Shattered Lives
Children Who Live with Courage and Dignity
Camila Batmanghelidjh
ISBN 1 84310 434 2

Working with Anger and Young People
Nick Luxmoore
ISBN 1 84310 466 0

Listening to Young People in School, Youth Work
and Counselling
Nick Luxmoore
ISBN 1 85302 909 2

Working with Gangs and Young People
A Toolkit for Resolving Group Conflict
Jessie Feinstein and Nia Imani Kuumba
ISBN 1 84310 447 4

Therapeutic Approaches in Work with Traumatised
Children and Young People
Theory and Practice
Patrick Tomlinson
ISBN 1 84310 187 4

The Time of the Therapeutic Communities
People, Places and Events
Liam Clarke
ISBN 1 84310 128 9

Valuing and Educating Young People

Stern Love the Lyward Way

Jeremy Harvey

Foreword by Tim Brighouse

Jessica Kingsley Publishers
London and Philadelphia

First published in 2006
by Jessica Kingsley Publishers
116 Pentonville Road
London N1 9JB, UK
and
400 Market Street, Suite 400
Philadelphia, PA 19106, USA

www.jkp.com

Library of Congress Cataloging in Publication Data
Harvey, Jeremy, 1938-
  Valuing and educating young people : stern love the Lyward way / Jeremy Harvey ;
Foreword by Tim Brighouse.
     p. cm.
  Includes bibliographical references.
  ISBN-13: 978-1-84310-056-0 (pbk. : alk. paper)
  ISBN-10: 1-84310-056-8 (pbk. : alk. paper) 1. Problem children--Education--England.
  2. Youth with social disabilities--Education. 3. Lyward, George, 1894-1973. I. Title.
  LC4803.G7H37 2006
  371.930941--dc22

                              2006005658

British Library Cataloguing in Publication Data
A CIP catalogue record for this book is available from the British Library

ISBN-13: 9 78 1 84 310 0560
ISBN-10: 1 84310 0568

Printed and bound in Great Britain by
Athenaeum Press, Gateshead, Tyne and Wear

In memory of

Syd Hopkins 1919–1999
Roy Niblett 1906–2005
George Rickey 1906–2002

Humble giants and educators
through conversation

The author and publisher gratefully acknowledge the permission granted to reproduce the copyright material in this book.

Extract on page 13 from Storytelling, Imagination and Faith by William J. Bausch, published by Twenty-Third Publications. Reproduced by permission of Twenty-Third Publications.

Extract on page 20 by Frances Spalding, first published in The Independent, 15 August 2001. Copyright © Frances Spalding. Reproduced by permission of The Independent.

Extracts on pages 20 and 42 from The Boy with No Shoes by William Horwood, published by Hodder Headline. Reproduced by Permission of Hodder Headline Limited.

Extract on page 36 by Philip Beadle, copyright © Guardian Newspapers Limited. Reproduced by Permission of Guardian Newspapers Limited.

Poem on pages 75–6 'Learning to Wait' by Richard Church. Reproduced by permission of Pollinger Limited and the proprietor.

Extract on pages 82–3 from J. Prickett, 'A Memorial Address', New Era, 55, 3, reproduced by permission of New Era, now New Era in Education, published since 1921 by the World Education Fellowship (WEF), www.newerasineducation.co.uk.

Extract on page 93 from Life Education Discovery: A Memoir and Selected Essays by Roy Niblett, published by Pomegranate Books, Bristol. Reproduced by permission of Pomegranate Books.

Extract on page 93 from Nature Cure by Richard Mabey, published by Chatto and Windus. Reprinted by permission of The Random House Group Ltd.

Poem on pages 98–9 'Born Yesterday' by Philip Larkin, reprinted from The Less Deceived by permission of The Marvell Press, England and Australia.

Extract on pages 130–1 from S. Roberts, 'Glimpses into the Community', New Era, 55, 3, reproduced by permission of New Era, now New Era in Education, published since 1921 by the World Education Fellowship (WEF), www.newerasineducation.co.uk.

Every reasonable effort has been made to trace copyright holders and to obtain their permission for the use of copyright material. The author apologizes for any errors or omissions in the above list and would be grateful for notification of any corrections or additions. Every effort will be made to promptly incorporate them in future reprints or editions of this book.

Contents

Foreword

This book is about a visionary educationalist, an extraordinary educator, an outstanding teacher and an inspired and successful social worker. It's unusual enough to meet any one of these characters, but to find a combination of all four in one individual is rare indeed. Yet that's what George Lyward was. An educationalist I'm defining here as someone with a wider view of some part of education provision – with a view of 'what is' and 'what might be' that transcends their immediate context if you like. The educator is someone who shoulders the responsibility to help create autonomous learners. The social worker is keen to ensure that an individual can operate successfully as a human being within society. The teacher is the focused skilled practitioner who knows the secret of what Thring described as:

> St Augustine's golden key, which though it be of gold is useless unless it fits the wards of the lock. And I found the wards I had to fit, the minds of those little street boys very queer and tortuous affairs they were too. So I had to set about cutting and chipping myself into the shape of a wooden key which however common it might look should have the one merit of a key, the merit of unlocking the mind and opening the shut chambers of the heart.

Like Thring, Lyward chose a very challenging set of youngsters to teach, educate and set on life's path. Unlike Thring, who started in the back streets of a big city but went on to found the public school Uppingham, Lyward spent almost a lifetime working with successive generations of very challenging youngsters whom the rest of the system had given up on. He founded a school community at a house bought for the purpose, Finchden Manor, near Tenterden in Kent. It turned out to be an extraordinarily successful educational and therapeutic community.

In these pages we glimpse some of the essentials of the outstanding teacher. First, you treat the teaching group as a collective identified with the teacher by the all embracing 'we' – 'We can crack this algebraic problem together class 9: it's tough but together we can do it' – while simultaneously treating every individual in a unique and personal way. Second, you are safely unpredictable to those you teach. Third, you have to believe – really believe – that every one of those you teach can succeed and not be too bothered about the speed at which this success comes. Fourth, you are always prepared to walk the extra miles for each and every one of them while expecting the group as a whole to do the same for their fellow pupils. Fifth, you will never confuse great effort on the part of a pupil as a sign of their lack of ability. Sixth, you will always regard a child's failure to learn as a challenge to your own ability to teach successfully and a spur to extend your own skill. Finally, you are hospitable, warm and accurate with frequent praise while being sparing but precise and constructive with criticism.

There is however much else to learn in this book, not just from and about Lyward and his beliefs and practices. Jeremy Harvey, himself an extraordinary educator, cleverly cross-references the points he makes about Lyward's philosophy and practice with film, prose, poetry and other examples drawn from pioneering adventures in education like Summerhill. Jeremy Harvey knows from his own career, most of it having occurred before the stifling impact of the National Curriculum took effect, what it is to take risks and innovate and, most importantly, to have the time and of course the inclination to provide for pupils what he calls 'hospitality' – or safety with rigour, forgiveness with expectation, humour with serious intent – which all good teachers provide for their pupils and to which, if the teacher is outstanding, so many pupils respond. They rise to the challenge.

If you want to learn more of this and be both reminded of why teaching is the most important job in the world and catch glimpses of the magic teachers weave, read on. Moreover, it is particularly appropriate that the book is coming out when the Every Child Matters agenda is so prominent in the UK. Its emphasis on education combined with social services taking on wider responsibilities for children at local authority level will make the book especially relevant now. It will be relevant too to all those who share all or part of Lyward's agenda in whatever country they live.

Tim Brighouse
March 2006

Acknowledgements

With thanks for past conversations

During the early 1980s I used to talk to Syd Hopkins about George Lyward whom he had been helped by and worked with. Those conversations led to my finding out about Lyward's life and writings in the second half of the decade. Syd started me on my journey. The many conversations, letters and papers received, and help given by so many, were gratefully acknowledged in the resulting thesis (Harvey 1991).

Friendships also stemmed from that decade of Lywardian exploration. Jill Hopkins gave me much time and hospitality. She passed on material and ideas and introduced me to Jessica Kingsley. This book emerged from conversations with both.

George Rickey, the kinetic sculptor, wrote from the United States to tell me how much he owed to Lyward's teaching at Glenalmond, and we corresponded and met in London and New York state. He sent letters and photos from his huge personal archive and he was very generous in many other ways. Professor Roy Niblett shared his recollections of Lyward in the 1950s, lent books and articles, recommended the *Audenshaw Papers* and networked for me. His amazing capacity to live actively in the present, through his nineties, kept me alert and curious.

With thanks for more gifts and conversations

In the compiling of this book there are others who gave me, or let me use, additional material, lent me books and gave practical help, especially Tim Baddeley, Michael Burn, Fiona Colbert and St John's College, Cambridge; Jennifer Cole, who translated the Rilke letter for me; Gay Drysdale, Craig Fees and the PETT archive; Alex Findlater, Greg Gardner, William Gorge, Jake Lever, Roland Niblett, Liz Owen, Christopher Richards, Sallie Roberts, Tom Robinson, Rod Salter, Mike Turner and Martin Whinney.

I have also had fruitful conversations and/or correspondence with Gerald Baddeley, Jon Broad, Adrian Campbell, Elizabeth Corner, Brian Cresswell, John Cross, Mary Earl, Craig Fees, Helen Frye, Mike Golby, Henry Haslam, Roger Harcourt, John Scott Hart, John Lyward, Stella Marshall, Mike Matthews, Allen Perrott, Tom Preater, Jack Priestley, Harry Procter, Sigurd Reimers, Jon Rose, Rowan Williams and James Willis.

Craig Fees suggested we set up a support group to get me writing about Lyward. That became the Obridge group which has had papers written for it on many educational subjects, the conversations about which have been valuable and enjoyable.

My family, especially my wife Sheila, has had to live with my fascination with Lyward and with the slow gestation of my understanding of his ideas and of my writing. Their acceptance of this has been crucial, as has been their readiness to wait. My thanks to them for their suggestions.

Having to wait has also been the fate of Professor Tim Brighouse, who promised years ago to write the foreword. I thank him for that, and also for all he does to enable teachers to teach well and for his inspirational contribution to education.

Writing a book is inevitably a solitary occupation. I have enjoyed the advice and guidance of my editors Leonie Sloman, Ruth Ballantyne and Alison McCullough, as well as their willingness to help sort out some of the conundrums.

In hopes of further conversations

Much of the gestation of this book has happened through internal conversations that I have had with the material and with myself. In addition to these musings, it should be clear that I owe much to past and present conversations. I am now looking forward to future ones – and to the possibility of hearing from others who knew Lyward.

The book inevitably presents one point of view for which I take full responsibility. Any errors are mine. If you would like to converse about anything in the book, or can correct something, my email is jersheharvey@aol.com

Obridge House
February 2006

CHAPTER 1

Meeting Mr Lyward

To be a person is to have a story. (Bausch 2002, p.171)

'Don't give me lip!'

I had to go to our local corner shop the other day. When I arrived I found a group of youngsters from the local secondary school were chatting and blocking the entrance. I made my way through them and as I did the manager appeared and asked them to keep the entrance clear. One of them answered back, mimicking him. 'Don't give me any of that lip!' snapped the man, and he moved them right away from the forecourt.

That incident reminded me of George Lyward and his way of getting the young to work with him rather than – unnecessarily – getting their backs up.

Had I been the shop manager, adopting a Lywardian approach, I would have ignored that momentary answering back while still insisting politely and firmly that they did not block the entrance. If I had reacted to that answering back, not only would I have played into the hands of the boys who had been hoping to wind me up, but I would then have had to use my power, my adult position, to insist that he and his friends did as I told them. To achieve that, I would probably have had to raise my voice, glare at them and stay there until they had gone away. For it would have become a situation which I had to win and they had to lose.

By getting them to do what I needed them to do – so my imaginary intervention has it – without my having to get cross, the possibility was there for our next meeting (either with that boy or with the group) to be friendly enough and even a bit deeper. The relationship

Lyward was seeking in his contacts with young people, and with adults, was one based on trust and mutual respect, on a deep awareness of their common humanity.

Who was Lyward? Why should I turn to him for guidance? And why should I write about him?

A teacher through and through

Lyward was born in south London in 1894 in the late Victorian period. His mother was a primary school teacher. His father was a musician, an opera singer by night and a clerk by day. He was a restless man who was later to leave his wife and their four children. Lyward was the younger of twins and he was expected to be chivalrous to his eldest sister, Polly. He grew up the only male in a female household which, in addition to his two younger sisters, included two aunts. The 1901 census records him living in Battersea in a household of eight with his father listed as resident.

Financially the family struggled, but managed to get by.

George was a lonely and rather sickly child who nearly died of polio when he was six. His interests were reading and playing the piano, which he would practise for hours. For this and his general frailty, he was teased both at school and in the street, and so he took to reading in the public library (Prickett 1974).

He went to Emanuel School where he fitted in happily enough. He was noticed by the staff when, at the age of 16, despite the after-effects of polio, he elected to play rugby, and so risked serious injury. He was made a prefect and put in charge of the lower fifth form, known to the staff as 'the toughs'. Some members of this form were bigger than he was, but they did as he requested.

At the age of 18, six weeks after leaving school, George became a teacher in a prep school in Wandsworth Common. He recalled standing in front of the class and thinking, 'We are in this together. We are members one of the other. That is the most important thing about this moment.' It was a discovery that was to shape his thinking for the rest of his life.

He wanted to go to university but first he had to qualify. And so he became an external student of King's College, London, attending evening classes for the next five years. By day he taught: in several more prep schools, then briefly at Kingston Grammar, before joining the staff of his own former school, Emanuel.

Eighteen months later, in 1917, he won a choral exhibition to St John's, Cambridge, and chose to read history. He was able to afford to take up his place thanks to a grant from an ordination fund.

It was a time of sheer joy. He was a bass in the college choir and in several of its musical societies, and he sang solos and song cycles in college concerts. He became junior treasurer, then secretary of the College Mission which helped boys in south London, and for his last two years he was tutor of School House and rugby coach at the Perse School, Cambridge. He was billeted with the bachelor headmaster and scholar, Dr Rowse.

He lived frugally, running up a total college bill of £71 – that was under half the estimated average for the time. His scholarship was worth a total of £90 and he also received small subsidies reserved for needy students. The Perse job helped him to pay his way.

He left Cambridge intending to become a priest in the Church of England. He obtained a grant to pay for his training and began attending Cheshunt College, a theological college. But he withdrew from there a few weeks before he would have been ordained a deacon. He was unhappy because he thought that the Church worshipped a transcendent God who was seen as high and mighty, lifted up, out of reach. Lyward felt that a balance had been lost since such looking-up ignored the immanence of God, that of God which was inside each person.

He remained reluctant to talk about why he rejected ordination. He retained a strong but private faith, keeping his beliefs to himself. He kept away from church buildings claiming that he lost all sense of God every time he went inside one.

He turned his back on organized religion, yet many have described him as a very spiritual person. He was fond of quoting from the Bible and he wrote at least one play in which Christ featured as the Word made flesh, and he talked and wrote persuasively about Love as the mystery at the heart of our lives. Years later he kept referring to the mystery within Finchden Manor.

He returned to teaching, once more to Emanuel – for a two-year spell as head of English – then moved to Trinity College, Glenalmond, in Scotland where the new warden, Matheson, appointed him head of the modern sixth. His task was to raise standards, a job he tackled with enormous energy and creativity. In the company of other new staff, including the Olympic athelete and musician, William Seagrove, who became a close friend, Lyward helped Matheson to modernize the school.

Just as Cambridge had been a very happy time, so Glenalmond was also. He had the teaching job he relished – and in a school where he felt high standards could be achieved. Thanks to his drive and ordered and imaginative way of teaching, standards soon rose in history. He had an impact across the culture of the college. Drama flourished, as did music. Lyward and Seagrove got an orchestra together. The school rugby team began to win matches, and the staff put on plays and musical evenings in which he often took part. He also wrote and produced three verse plays. He planned to write at least one textbook. However, his large workload increased when he became housemaster of the new junior house (for which he appointed the American George Rickey, the future artist and kinetic sculptor, to be his first prefect). He seemed destined for higher things and at one stage was in the running for two headships.

Unfortunately he had driven himself too hard, trying to achieve much in too short a time; after breaking off his engagement to marry, he suffered a severe breakdown in early 1928 and left Glenalmond without any formal goodbyes – though there was a warm but short tribute in the school magazine.

He reflected on his years of teaching after rejecting ordination thus. 'It was a crowded life and so not unhappy. But teaching can be a way of avoiding growing pains. I was never completely doped by glowing testimonials and at last I found myself sufficiently released from the fear of plunging out.' (Lyward 1937b, p.186).

'Plunging out' meant gradually becoming his own person and trusting his own judgement. Later this emerged as tackling pioneering work with boys who were on the educational scrapheap. But first, over the two years after his breakdown, he suffered much, initially being able to do very little. He feared his teaching days were over. He experienced a frightening wilderness period, doubting he was capable of doing anything, and living as if in a dark cloud, which only began to lift when he was admitted to a nursing home run by Dr Crichton-Miller.

Under the skilful care of three doctors he became well enough to help, at their request, other patients. One of these patients, Max Warren, afterwards wrote (1974) that he owed his recovery from being near to death to Lyward's ministrations.

One May day in 1930 at the suggestion of Dr Rees, one of his doctors, Lyward set out with two older boys and a colleague, Stephen Williamson, for the Guildables, a farm near Edenbridge. A cow accompanied them. While Stephen ran the farm with help from the boys, Lyward cared for their emotional and educational needs. This was the beginning of the work he would do for the rest of his life, for the next 43 years. He would be 'teaching', yet for much of the time not formally teaching.

Within five years the number of boys had expanded from two to 20, and Lyward had married Sadie, a red-haired sculptress whom he had met at Easter in Cromer in 1931. They had a son, John, and when the owner wanted the Guildables back, they found and bought – for £5000 – rambling, rundown Finchden, an Elizabethan manor on the outskirts of Tenterden in Kent. They moved there in May 1935.

Apart from having to evacuate it during the war, the Lywards remained at Finchden for the rest of their lives. Sadie died in the mid-1960s, Lyward in 1973 aged 79, still 'chief' of the community that he had so lovingly created. Thanks to Michael Burn's *Mr. Lyward's Answer* (1956) Finchden had become both well known and much visited and, in addition, Lyward was in demand as a lecturer. He became an external examiner and occasional lecturer in special education for Bristol University. Invited to preach in Westminster Abbey by Max Warren, he chose not to give a sermon but to talk about Finchden. He was awarded the OBE which was in acknowledgement of his unusual and remarkable work.

At his memorial service in St Martin's in the Fields in October 1973, a large congregation, which included many well-known and successful people, gathered to pay their respects to a beloved teacher, father figure and friend. Many knew that he had helped them turn their lives round. Tom Robinson (2003b) recalls the surprise engendered among those present when they recognized someone whom they had not hitherto known was at Finchden.

Such affection and respect, such recognition of what one owes to a particular teacher, is not unique to Lyward. It has existed as long as there has been teaching and I expect it to be ever thus. Many of us can claim to have been taught by a beloved teacher but do we let the teacher know and do we tell others about him or her? Good teaching is always worthy of being announced from the rooftops or by letter or email.

What Finchden stood for

In his 43 years of running Finchden Manor as a community Lyward specialized in caring for intelligent and emotionally damaged young boys from 14 upwards, offering them respite or relaxation from the pressures, nagging and unhelpful expectations which had dogged them. Why were they there? They had failed to 'succeed' in the eyes of their teachers or parents or society. Writing of Finchden Manor, he said:

> We do not stand for 'freedom' or 'self-expression', because 'freedom' can sometimes be a grievous burden and 'self-expression' mere vomiting. We are concerned with providing security within which release and re-education can come to those who have pulled down the shutters on themselves or bitten society. Our co-operations, unfairnesses, impingements and distinctions are those characteristic of life rather than those characteristic of so many institutions; and they are experienced within adequate security. (1937b, p.186)

Notice the 'we'. Lyward was writing *from within* the community. Any changes, any successful re-educating, or 're-weaning', as he also described it, would take place as a result of the combined efforts of staff and boys. The boys had pulled down the shutters of life, shut up their shop or bitten society; taken their anger and disappointment and frustrations out on others.

Lyward gave these boys time enough. He waited with them until they were ready to re-open their shutters and to rejoin life outside Finchden.

Meeting Mr Lyward

Having introduced Lyward, who he was and what he achieved, I need to explain my interest in him. I came across him second-hand and by accident.

In the early 1960s I was a student at Cuddesdon theological college when one evening Ben de la Mare, a fellow student, lent me *Mr. Lyward's Answer* by Michael Burn. I had never heard of either Lyward or Burn but I thanked Ben, and read the book.

That apparently random lending of a book and my reading of it changed my life's direction. That reading tipped me out of ordination (which I was not sure about, anyway) and into teaching. Before then I had been attracted by one kind of teaching only – by tutoring: the process of having one-to-one conversations about the subject being studied with ample time to develop ideas, ask questions and search for answers. It was an open-ended, vigorous and largely unthreatening process.

But thanks to *Mr. Lyward's Answer* I found myself wishing I had been taught by teachers as sympathetic and understanding as Lyward and – to my surprise – I began to want to teach in a school, and to teach in a Lywardian way.

I never met George Lyward, whom I shall refer to as Lyward, but his way of working with young people has had a powerful effect on me. What he practised, as vividly described by Burn in his superb book, was, I felt sure, suitable and adaptable for any teaching I might one day do; and if for me, then why not also for teachers in any kind of classroom?

CHAPTER 2

Conditions
of successful learning

All true appreciations of people are bound to be blurred, finding a bit here, a bit there – it's all approximate. (Michael Andrews, cited in Spalding 2001, p.16)

The strong help the weak: that's the beginning and end of things so far as a community goes. (Granny to Jimmy in The Boy with No Shoes, *Horwood 2004, p.253)*

'Etre et avoir'

Teaching is a craft, and good teachers take care to have their room ready, know their material and adapt it to their class's readiness. Monsieur Lopez, the French primary school teacher featured in the film *Etre et Avoir* (Philibert, 2002), prepares meticulously for his lessons. As part of that he arranges his room in readiness for the children's arrival, moving a chair and placing an open book by a child's place. That child can then come in, greet her teacher, sit down and get straight into her work.

Monsieur Lopez also keeps a very orderly room in which there is a place for everything. His wall displays are tidy and he places the work tables close to the blackboards so that it is easy for the younger children to get up and write on them. He has established a reading area which has a comfortable sofa in it. He has successfully created the physical conditions in which his pupils can get on with their tasks and learn contentedly.

But there is much more to his teaching than that. In particular he relates to each member of the class, talking to each for several minutes at a time while they are on task. First he notes what they had done and checks whether they understand it, maybe reminding them of the techniques involved, and then he helps them to master the rest of the task.

Lopez enables them to be themselves and to learn at their best speed. He also gives them support and encouragement while demanding even more effort and achievement. If the children wish to sit back and relax, he challenges such opting out. With Lopez they can truly be (*etre*) and have (*avoir*) but they cannot opt out.

'We are all people together'

Lyward equally sought to create the conditions for successful learning, which included being aware of the emotional needs of young people, both in his teaching in the 1920s (before his breakdown) and in his work in the 1930s (after it). Yet he would appear to have been as much concerned about the right psychological approach, which included establishing that he and his class were members one of another, as getting the classroom layout right. We know more about his concern for a young person's emotional development and his philosophy of education than about his classroom arrangements. Unlike Monsieur Lopez he was never filmed while teaching.

The key idea, the foundation of all his work, came to him very early in his career. It was not something he had been told. It came as a sudden realization. He was 18 years old and he was standing before a class of children for the first time. He recalled that revelation 57 years later (Lyward 1970, pp 17–18):

> The thought came to me, almost like a blow, 'These are people – we are all people together in a room – that is the most important fact about this situation.' That they were my pupils (with emphasis on both words) was a secondary fact completely dwarfed by the first almost alarming realization.

The first and most important thing, Lyward realized, was that he and his class were people together in one room, sharing a common humanity. They needed each other and they belonged to each other. One consequence of this awareness was:

> that I was prepared from the start to take into account the possible fears, guilt, perfectionism, self-pity (and so on) which so many of the pupils brought with them to school from their homes and their earlier lives, and which affected their approach to the subjects of the curriculum. (Lyward 1970, p.18)

There was another element to this discovery and it concerned his expectations of them which he decided must be realistic rather than perfectionistic.

> [it] meant that I never again valued quantity too highly, or troubled about 'mistakes', or facts forgotten the next day, or interruptions, or 'talking in class', or momentary impertinences. Nothing could separate us: <u>we were members one of another</u>. (Prickett 1974, p.54)

What counted above all else was their membership of the human race; they were people on a journey together. And since they were travelling together, they must keep together, look after each other and not get momentary things, such as one person's industry, another's idleness or another's cheek, out of proportion by seeing them as too important or too awful.

I suggested that the corner-shop story of a momentary impertinence, with which I began this book, was one such occasion when Lyward would not have over-reacted. The thinking – our membership one of another – is biblical and can be found, for instance, in Romans XII: 4–5. The argument is that Christians, though very different as persons, are made one, 'are one body', by their belonging to Christ. As a result of this they are responsible for each other. They are 'individually members one of another' (Revised Standard Version).

Some may object to the Christian source of Lyward's insight and yet accept it from another conceptual route. Others might argue that such an approach only applies if you hold a Christian understanding of others. But Lyward believed that it applied to us all, whatever our faith or lack of it. To Lyward this awareness of our common membership of this planet, and our resulting dependence on and responsibility for each other, was fundamental. John Donne expressed the same truth when he meditated that 'No man is an island entire of itself' (Scott 1997, p.75). Whether we like it or not, we are our brother's and sister's keeper.

This belonging to each other, and not just to our family, brings obligations and benefits. They both tie and free us. Secure in that knowledge we can attend to our work and our duties (the things only we can do) and also relax and have fun, comforted by being aware that we are – in some inexplicable and mysterious way – linked together consciously and even more so at an unconscious level; and that, if such membership is realized in, say, a class or team, then while being aware of ourselves, our uniqueness, we can also feel that we belong to the others. They in turn increasingly know that they need us. We belong to each other.

Where does competition fit into this strong emphasis on our membership one of another? Should it be banned as pulling against such membership? It is partly inevitable that someone wants to be the best within a group, and it is human nature to make comparisons. For instance, I may note that someone has an aptitude for computing and keyboard skills while knowing that I do not. But once I accept the other's talent and skill and see it as part of our difference, then I can let that person be and even encourage their further development of that aptitude. I do not have to become competitive about our different levels of computer literacy.

Fulfilling one's potential in any aspect of life need not be at the expense of denying others their chance to do the same and to develop their gifts and interests. It is part of the teacher's calling to encourage individual aspiration and ambition while protecting the general welfare and interests of the class. Through skilful nurturing an ethos can arise which welcomes difference, success and different speeds of achievement; which allows competition especially when it is unavoidable but also keeps it subordinate to the bigger truth that we need and depend on each other. The class or group, large or small, when well cared for, is a good medium for keeping that balance and for enabling everyone to flourish.

It is also extremely catching and infecting, in the best sense, when a person who is very good at something is modest and gracious about his or her achievements.

The desert fathers and mothers of the Christian church (Williams 2003), who had fled the Egyptian towns for the desert in the early centuries of the Christian church, understood that they would die were it not for their neighbour, their fellow town-fleer. The wise among them knew that they could not survive on their own. Each needed the help of a neighbour in order to survive. And vice versa. Each of us is our neighbour's keeper, hard as it is to live by that.

Lyward put this realization into practice. So did Monsieur Lopez. And so do many other teachers – though by no means all!

Instances of realizing our membership

It is possible to show we value the other person in our class or school in a range of ways, and the valuing does not have to come solely from the teacher. In *Etre et Avoir* at the end of the summer term there was a formal and affectionate act of goodbye at the school door. For two of the boys it was their goodbye to the school, for they were moving to the middle school. As the class left Monsieur Lopez kissed each pupil on each cheek and was in turn kissed back. He had to stoop to do so.

Such may be the custom in France, especially in small rural primary schools. If that is so it could be dismissed as ritual, as a customary response. But it was more than that. It marked affection and respect by the children for their teacher, and was part of their way of saying 'thank you'. For his part he was wishing them well, thanking them for their cooperation, and returning them to their families for the long holiday. Such a practice movingly expressed and summed up their feelings for one another.

Now in other countries, for example, in the UK, USA and Canada, Australia and New Zealand, we are very unlikely to act like that and we may consider the French are going over the top. Kiss a teacher a formal goodbye! That's far too demonstrative. Yet Lopez's practice does support those who argue (such as Salzberger-Wittenburg, Henry and Osborne 1983) that some form of recognition of the school year's end is important as endings are significant to us all, and children especially need there to be some recognition that the school year is over. Beginnings (such as the start of a term or a move to a new school) and endings (such as leaving a school) are much harder for children – and staff – than is generally realized.

Schools have their own way of acknowledging the start and finish of term. Classroom and form teachers will also have their preferred ways of welcoming children and sending them off for the holidays or to join another school. What Lopez does is to make sure that the significance of these endings is marked in such a way that includes every child.

For those of us not wishing to adopt Lopez's practice one way of marking such ends of term and of the school year would be for the head/form/class teacher to shake hands with each boy and girl as they leave for the holidays.

Saying it with flowers

The Russians have a way of marking the end of the summer break and the beginning of the school year, which also serves to express their sense of membership one of another. Adam Nicolson in St Petersburg noticed one Sunday evening early in September that families returning to the city by car and tram were bearing 'orange and blood-red dahlias and purple and pink gladioli'. The next morning it became clear why:

> from eight o'clock onwards, the pavements of the city, the embankments alongside the canals were filled with rivers of children walking to school for the first day of term, all with an enormous bunch of these flowers in their hands.
> At the school doors, the teachers stood like opera divas, receiving the tributes from their pupils, the headmistresses drowning in the biggest bunches, gardenfuls of flowers clustered to the bosom. It felt like the most exciting fiesta, the beginning of school, the end of summer. (2003, p.20)

A cynic might say that the parents were using flowers as a bribe to please their child's teacher or headmistress. Another observer might note that such gestures have become traditional, the norm, and that as a result it is hard for any family to break such a tradition which may have become long outmoded and which may hide real feelings.

But even if the motives of those St Petersburg parents were suspect and their reactions mechanical, who knows the benefits that seasonal gift brings in the way of enhancing the teachers' sense of membership with their pupils and vice versa? Giving and receiving are ways of allowing us to express our feelings for the other. And within the children's feelings surely there will be hopes, dreams and troublesome fears? The Russian custom draws family, child and teacher closer at the start of a new school year. That is highly desirable – especially if a teacher and class can start the year with more smiles rather than apprehension.

Addressing the one and the many

If each person is special and unique, then he/she needs to be taught in a way that addresses his or her particular needs and learning strengths. That is an irrefutable axiom. But it is also an impossible ideal to achieve, I hear some teachers saying. All right, it might be possible in a one-to-one tutorial or in Monsieur Lopez's small primary class, they concede, but it is virtually ruled out when you have a large class of pupils. How can, say, a primary teacher with 30 or more infants address each one's needs and also teach them the basic core skills that the National Curriculum requires? Even worse, how can an infant teacher tick the 117 assessment boxes on each child (which they are required to do) and have time and energy for their next day's preparation?

Granted that a one-to-one session once a week, say, is a very good way of meeting an individual's learning needs, how can one manage that kind of rhythm of individual help within a large class? I will address that in a moment. First let me cite the experience of Tony Mooney (2004), an experienced science and maths teacher now specializing in one-to-one home tutoring. He has found that teenagers will respond to private coaching regardless of the kind of school (state or private) they are at, according to their ability; simply because Mooney is providing them with time to ask about and sort out the things that confuse them or that they cannot understand. His tutees thrive on being given individual help and attention. And, without doubt, on the talk and conversation that is generated.

Mooney notes that middle-class parents pay for private schooling because their child will be taught in small classes and for home tutoring because he or she will get individual attention. What helps a boy or girl to succeed, Mooney argues, is not particularly the small class size or the quality of private school teaching, which can be much worse than in a state school, but the fact that someone is giving their child a weekly slot of undivided attention during which his or her learning and emotional needs are being addressed.

Suppose Mooney is right: that does not necessarily mean that such undivided attention on one person can be built into the ordinary life of larger classes. Lyward argued that it could. He believed that individual attention and one-to-one support could be included and incorporated into classroom teaching without the many getting out of control or being neglected. (Chapter 3 looks at the sort of discipline and relationships needed to achieve that.)

He saw all schoolteaching as having to balance the needs of the one person with those of the many. He used several ways of focusing on one boy: for instance when he spoke to that boy; when he wrote a comment to him or marked his work; when he enabled the boy to speak to him or to others, such as when he answered a question or read a poem; when he invited the boy to do a job, such as to fetch the form's register or to collect in or give out the class's exercise books; and when he wrote about the boy to another colleague or to his parents. He would also keep careful records of each person's progress. And he would make time for individual conversations which might happen as he walked round the room or by calling a boy up to his desk, while the rest of the class was engaged in some writing or study. Such conversations might happen around the school during casual moments or when a teacher and pupils were engaged in a joint activity such as a rehearsal.

Much of the routine stuff of classroom teaching includes many regular opportunities to relate to each boy and girl. The trick is to see that each of these interactions is significant and that then cumulatively helps the child to feel special and appreciated.

Equally a teacher has many opportunities to address and work with the many, with the whole class or group. Each of these contacts and interactions can also be made significant. It is a matter of seizing the whole-class moments to get the many to work well together while also helping each person to feel that he/she still matters; of balancing the work one does with the one and the many.

That it worked for Lyward, that he managed to look after the one and the many, is clear from a signed tribute he received in 1961 from members of a class he had taught in the 1920s. They had met again at a school reunion and they sent a signed menu card and this message to Lyward:

> From 2B 1916: 'We wish you to know that we will not forget – ever – former years. All of us (at the annual dinner) had one thing in common – a profound respect for your teaching and your influence on all our lives.' (Lyward 1970, p.18)

The 'All of us' and the 'all our lives' convey the breadth and the depth of Lyward's teaching and influence on them.

Teaching is a form of hospitality

At Finchden Manor in Kent Lyward likened his work in the second half of his career to practising a form of hospitality. He worked with boys from the age of 14 onwards and young men up to their early twenties who had been referred to him by psychiatrists, doctors, headteachers and other professionals as being unable to cope in school or in trouble with the police. Many were unwanted at school, by society or even by their families.

Because of what they had already been through and the emotional damage done to them (for instance by the continual rejection they had suffered), Lyward knew that to subject them to more traditional schooling would lead to a further and probably worsening sense of failure for each boy. But how to provide an answer for their current needs? How to start addressing the emotional damage that they had suffered? He was clear that conventional methods of schooling had failed this group.

So he created a residential community, which grew to about 40 boys in size, and he insisted that it was not a school in the accepted sense. He was right. It was an original, a true one-off creation, tailor-made for the apparent 'failures' who came to it.

It differed from an ordinary school in that there were no formal daily lessons for each member. Subjects were eventually studied and exams were then taken (by most boys) but only when the young man in question was judged ready for sustained study. Monthly reports were written and sent home and observations and notes of what a boy had said or done were put in his file as an ongoing record of his needs and progress.

Such a way of life, such a ruling out of studying until the right moment had come, meant that the members had to find something to do during the day when they were not doing their share of the chores, such as cooking or seeing that the boiler was properly stoked. For many it was to be some years before they were deemed ready to study in any formal way.

Meanwhile what Finchden did offer them was a form of hospitality, a home, a respite from false and harmful pressures, a chance to recover before leaping forward (the French refer to 'reculer pour mieux sauter': stepping back the better to jump forward) and space to be.

For those who were ready there were lessons in subjects such as maths, English, history, science and foreign languages. There was never any attempt to link a boy's age to his level of study. If he was 18 before he was ready to study, then that is when he began to study for, say, O levels. *Readiness* for study was the criterion, not age. Finchden followed the boy rather than, as largely still happens in maintained schools and many public schools, a person's age dictates the tests and exams he/she takes.

Lyward summed up Finchden's approach to teaching thus: 'the objective is to fit the teaching to the true age of those who are taught; to encourage the use of the brain according to its age limits' (Lyward, undated, p.3).

By 'true age' Lyward meant a boy's readiness for learning which included what his brain was ready for him to study. He argued that it was a waste of time to force a university-style education, as some of the public schools had been doing, on a boy's brains which were of pre-university age. Furthermore, unless education was education for living it was not going to match a youngster's needs: worse it might lead him to a nervous breakdown. Lyward had had to pick up the pieces of many of these.

He believed, too, that a forcing style of education, a cramming style of teaching, a 'you will study this because you have to – and it's good for you!' approach, if universally imposed, would threaten the breakdown of civilization. (Presumably he was referring to a potential breakdown in attitudes and a rejecting of traditional values in the United Kingdom first and foremost.)

What Lyward meant by education is summed up in Chapter 5, although aspects of his overall philosophy are examined in this chapter and the succeeding ones.

Providing time and space

The daily framework devised by Lyward for these boys, first at the Guildables and then at Finchden, was very simple: they were provided with four square meals a day. That was the hospitality on offer. Between these mealtimes and the chores they had to do there was plenty of time to follow any pursuits or interests that were available. Within this time to freewheel a boy might attempt to make a guitar or ask to be shown how a computer was constructed. He could also play football or cricket, which might lead to his playing for the Finchden team, or take part in the play that was being rehearsed. Lyward liked calling at short notice for a 'Command Performance', which meant an evening of music and drama.

A boy might well make music, on his own or with others. Burn (1956) recalled plenty of informal music-making going on throughout the building: Bach, Chopin and boogie-woogie being played on pianos, and elsewhere Lyward singing to a boy's accompaniment.

For the residents of Finchden both the frequent informal contact they had with staff, including Mr and Mrs Lyward, and the very ethos of the place, were also a form of hospitality. They were made welcome as if they were guests. But they were not guests. They were paying members of a community that focused on both their immediate and long-term educational needs. And when there were guests at Finchden – friends of Lyward or people who had asked to visit – then the boys were expected to be hosts and to make all guests and visitors feel welcome.

The hospitality experienced at Finchden was built round the giving of space, both physical and temporal, to each boy so that he could be left to find things to do that suited him within an atmosphere of care and support. Each boy was given gentle attention, not brusque criticism. He was welcomed and looked after as if he was an honoured guest, which he might feel he was, at first. More important though: he came to know he was part of a caring community.

To shout or not to shout

The boys were looked after by a staff who treated them courteously. For example the staff rarely shouted at a boy. Blandford (2004, p.10) believes that talking to others in a 'sensitive, respectful manner seems to encourage a sensitive, respectful response.' She was startled by the different feel she found in two schools she visited. In the first a senior member of staff shouted abuse at every child arriving at school. Although this teacher claimed that every child was valued, Blandford noted that all verbal communicating in that school was so noisy that shouting at someone was considered to be the norm.

In contrast in a neighbouring school 'staff and pupils spoke quietly to each other; they actually talked, listened and learned'.

As a new teacher I was advised by several people that if one shouts in the classroom, one is as good as admitting that one has lost control, and therefore that the class or the other person has won. Far better to keep one's voice down even if one has to indicate disapproval of what is going on.

And when I was a senior member of staff and had pupils sent to me for misbehaving, I also found that if I got angry and shouted at them, I would invariably later learn that the situation was not as grim or awful as had been depicted by staff: there were extenuating circumstances, facts which needed to be taken into account. Before blasting it would have been better to have checked more thoroughly by getting all aspects of the story.

On the other hand it has been quite clear at times that a temporary assumed anger – a teacher does need, at times, to be an actor – may be necessary to make it clear that certain actions or attitudes are unacceptable. A lesson has to be learnt quickly, when for instance people's safety or welfare is at risk. And sometimes there simply is not the time to postpone one's reaction: one has to trust a colleague's judgement and support their desire for good order in their classroom. It is better if these 'put on' moments of anger are rare and short-lived.

Just occasionally Lyward could be extremely cross, and at such times he was terrifying. This only happened when something serious had occurred. Then he would call a 'session', a gathering of all at Finchden, at which he made it clear what was unacceptable.

I doubt whether he was feigning anger on these occasions. A session was only called if he was extremely annoyed and felt he had to make it clear that there were limits. Once he had exploded, he usually relaxed and helped others to see that his wrath was over by deftly changing the subject or by a flash of wit which brought humour back into the room.

A good and wise leader needs to be aware of his or her dark or shadow side and of how he or she may accidentally or intentionally draw on it. That is part of the weight of being human. What matters in our contacts and relations with others is that we seek to use such moments, such flip-overs from control into wrath, as positively and creatively as possible. The danger is that in losing my temper I pass on the enormous destructive forces within me and so harm others. It is best for everyone's sake that such eruptions are rare. A school community does need to know, however, that there are limits which have to be observed for the good of all.

Returning to Finchden: the staff served the boys (by attending to their personal and psychological needs) and the boys in turn were expected to serve, wait on and do jobs for each other and also the staff. There was no punishment system and no sense of 'the staff are against us'.

However, to keep things fluid and to allow for a boy's emotional development, Lyward might respond to a boy's request unpredictably. The same request from two boys, for instance to go to the cinema, might well be treated differently: one boy being told he could go, the other he could not. This paradoxical treatment and these apparent unfairnesses were part of his deliberate attempt to keep attitudes and expectations fluid, to stop things getting fixed, and so, lifeless. They were a necessary way of responding to each boy according to his needs and his emotional readiness.

Visitors to Finchden were puzzled by, even provoked to protest about, his way of treating the boys in such a seemingly random, unfair way, and even with disdain when they asked for something. His relaxed and allegedly bizarre way of treating the boys is looked at in Chapter 3. In reality he believed that such a way of applying 'discipline' was helpful and creative and, furthermore, that he considered Finchden's approach to discipline would work well in ordinary schools.

High expectations – of fun!

The final ingredient in this Finchdonian form of hospitality was fun, and fun was on offer both around the place and in study times. There must be heaps of fun, Lyward always insisted.

When teaching at Emanuel School and at Trinity College, Glenalmond, he had worked his classes hard and expected his students to take their work seriously. It was only during his break-down, in the wilderness out-of-work years in the late 1920s, that he realized that he had pushed himself and others far too hard. At Glenalmond his slogan for himself and his students had been MOBED, which stood for My Own Best Efforts Doubled. The boys were frequently reminded that MOBED was expected of them.

In that respect his behaviour had bordered on the fanatic – though his intentions had always been to give his best to the college and the boys, and to get the best from those he taught and looked after.

He had, for instance, when coaching rugby, made junior boys get on their knees and kiss the turf as a sign of their submission to the game and of their readiness to give their all.

By the time Finchden was well established he had redressed the balance of his expectations for his pupils. He had become an enthusiastic advocate of the place of fun. Until they came to Finchden fun had been lacking from the lives of most of the boys. Instead they had experienced failure, been criticized and been starved of praise, put under far too much of the wrong kind of pressure and constantly nagged.

Each of those five ways of parents or teachers treating a child – failing to help him to achieve, constant cricitism, starving him of praise, piling on pressure and persistently nagging – can seriously damage a child's mental health. Combined they are lethal.

When a Finchden boy came down late for breakfast, knowing there was no cooked breakfast, Lyward might surprise him by asking the cook to give him one. Or Lyward might create fun out of the abuse of the 'no smoking in the bedrooms' rule. If he caught a boy smoking in bed, especially if he had warned him not to, he might on the second occasion douse him with a bucket of water in order to put the fire out!

This emphasis on the place of fun and the unexpected, of surprise both for pleasure and instruction, meant that nothing was allowed to become too serious, no attitudes were to become too fixed. The community's life was to remain fluid within a secure and expected framework of food and hospitality. Using a light touch in all his dealings with the boys was a core feature of Lyward's approach from the 1930s onwards.

Conversations on the hoof

Much of Lyward's 'teaching' was informal, away from the classroom. It happened out and about, indoors and outside. Wearing his trilby – a protection against catching a chill – he would wander round the house and grounds stopping to chat with this boy or that. A group might gather and he might challenge one boy about something, remind another of what he had promised to do, ask a question of a third and maybe tell a story, or call a member of staff to come and explain something. These moments would represent a form of peripatetic teaching, conversations on the hoof.

The boys would listen, respond, reflect. They knew they were not being judged. They knew that Lyward and his staff were on their side and were available when needed without their wishing to be too intrusive.

In this way both boys and staff could join in with any informal activities that happened to be going on, especially the things they were interested in, having fun in the process.

Being inspired by the community

This ambience of acceptance and hospitality in which the boys were enfolded helped them to experience good, or at least better, feelings about themselves and encouraged them to be open to new possibilities. Thus the boys gradually realized that they might not after all be failures or useless at everything. They became aware of how others around them were similar but different and also had to struggle if they were to change. And they began to believe that one day they could very well resume class lessons and undertake a course of study, and so make a return to the more publicly acceptable areas of education.

Lyward likened this process – of staying away from lessons, free-wheeling, before returning to formal study – as the boys' re-education.

In a published diary extract he explained:

> this is not a school in the usual sense of that word. It is a community of re-education (a clinic?) and I hold that most adolescents need more re-educating in their educating than they usually get. (Lyward 1937c, p.224)

It was not just the boys who ended up at Finchden that needed re-educating, Lyward felt. To illustrate what he considered as re-educating, he described how Ben (not his real name) had come to Finchden wearing glasses which were heavily tinted and had side pieces. Not long before he had arrived there Ben had declared that he could not manage without his glasses. This was against the advice of experts who had said he did not need glasses. Ben had insisted that he needed glasses and chose to have side pieces with his which made them look like blinkers.

One day these blinkers were accidentally broken and Ben declared that he did not want them mended. From that moment he did without glasses of any sort. Lyward's commentary on this development was that it had been obvious to the staff and the other 39 boys that he did not need them. It was clear that he had been hiding behind his blinkers, just as each of the other boys prior to their going to Finchden had been hiding behind something which had been their blinkers equivalent.

Among the things they had been hiding behind, Lyward noted, were expert knowledge, stupidity, top-of-the-class-itis, athletic skill, stealing and 'strong silence'. The latter was the resolve not to talk more than was essential – to annoy people by not answering them or joining in with ordinary conversation.

As regards stealing Lyward decided that all his boys had been stealing in one form or another. He did not mean that they had literally taken money from their parents or another person, though some had done that, but that they had all needed to take, both from others and from situations, what was not theirs – in order to survive.

Returning to Ben, Lyward declared that the other boys did not fuss because Ben was hiding behind a pair of ugly blinkers. That fact was obvious to them. And once Ben felt secure at Finchden, he gradually relaxed and conveyed by sign and tokens, 'I don't feel I need hide any longer *here*, but I can't climb down unaided.' At that time it was fitting that his glasses should break, with little said by him or those present other than the most casual references to the *fact* that this had happened.

In this same diary extract Lyward then added:

> Nobody enlarged upon the fact. Here, facts are allowed to speak for themselves, as facts have a way of doing in time when they are allowed to or are helped to by proper timing. I hope this story illustrates the supreme importance we attach to timing, which has nothing to do with our instinctive desire to 'do something about it now'. Living here is a great game, and good timing is the mark of good play. (1937c, p.224)

He liked to keep facts detached from feelings about them, and he often had to help parents understand the need to do this. When 'Robin Taylor' was at Finchden his father got behind on paying the fees, and Lyward suggested that the best solution was for Mr Taylor to pay a reduced fee. Mrs Taylor wrote to Lyward to say how embarrassed they felt about having to do this. To which Lyward replied that it was best to stick to the fact that the Taylors were behind on their payments, and for them and him to put personal feelings about this on one side. A new rate had been agreed which they could afford. It was best for them all that they now paid it, which they did.

That then left Robin to get on with his Finchden life and enabled the Taylors to stop worrying about the fees, and to continue to leave Robin in Lyward's care.

CHAPTER 3

Discipline which is creative

*A 'No' uttered from deepest conviction is better and greater than a
'Yes' merely offered to please, or, what is worse, to avoid trouble.
(Mahatma Ghandi, source unknown)*

*Praise is the surest, most positive, utterly foolproof way of keeping
a classroom of young people focused on the reason they are in the
classroom. (Philip Beadle 2005, p.10)*

Into a new world

Although it was not to become clear to them initially, Lyward offered
his Finchden newcomers a dramatic change of lifestyle: a settled form
of hospitality and a way of life based on a reduction of pressure, an
apparent absence of goals, and respite. Through these they were given
time to recover from the blows and buffets home, school and the wider
world had inflicted on them.

Dramatic change of another sort once happened to a friend, Greg.
He told my wife and me about it over breakfast two years ago when he
was about to return home. We had been talking about George Herbert
(Greg's journey would take him near to Bemerton, Herbert's parish
church and home) and that reminded him of his first significant
English lesson.

> I can't be sure but I think I remember my first English lessons
> with Roger [Harcourt]. I was nearly 15 years old. It was a
> grammar school. We were the second streamed class. We saw
> this new name on our timetable – Harcourt. A new teacher.
> Then arriving we picked up this was a young teacher. Not one

of the same old familiar faces. We thought we could have a bit of fun with him, play him up.

He gave out a sheet of short poems. It seemed a very odd way to start and we were a little intrigued. I cannot remember what the other poems were but I remember at the bottom of the sheet was 'Hope' by George Herbert (Hutchinson 1961, p.56).

> I gave to Hope a watch of mine; but he
>> An anchor gave to me.
> Then an old prayer book I did present:
>> And he an optic sent.
> With that I gave a vial full of tears:
>> But he a few green ears.
> Ah! Loiterer! I'll no more, no more I'll bring:
>> I did expect a ring.

He asked us to read all the short poems and then put them in the order that we liked them. I think someone said something like, 'You tell me, mate! How am I supposed to know!' It would have been said under the breath, for friends in the class to hear, not quite loud enough for the teacher to make out. But the implication would be plain: we are not playing your little game.

Roger handled it with total aplomb.

'You said?'

'What?'

'You said something. What did you say?'

Flushing scarlet.

'Tell us. It could be important. We want to hear your opinion.'

The boy blustered something, trying to fend off the unwanted attention he had brought upon himself, trying to retain some credibility but failing to do so. The new teacher, speaking quietly, moved on, back to the task. We were required to read the poems and then make our choices, which we preferred.

It is difficult to describe to younger people of another generation, what a revolutionary thing this was. We were not being instructed about the poems. That was what normally happened. We were being asked our opinion. From the very start. We were expected to know a good poem from a bad poem. Bad poems.

Now I suppose we tended to think that all poems were bad, that was OUR opinion. The teachers, we thought, believed that all poems were good. That was THEIR opinion. But here we were being brought into the debate.

That, and the way the smart remark had been handled, caused a small revolution. It all took place in the first ten minutes of the lesson. Then we were asked what we had noticed about the poems, and someone pitched in with a thought, then someone else, then someone else. The cynical ones, and we were all horny skinned cynics, suddenly found that they were a bit isolated and silly. This was an adult discussion. We could say what we liked. We could say a line in the poem was daft. We could say it was clever. Whatever we said was OK. As long as we were actually talking about the poem.

That had never happened before.

I remember thinking, before that revolutionary lesson, that English was a stupid subject. I mean, English! It was the language you spoke and thought in for Christ sake! What was the point of studying that? It was like studying walking! Our previous teacher had spent the last few weeks of the summer term introducing us to clause analysis: the art of taking sentences apart like a watch. That had in some small way impressed me: it made a simple subject into something difficult. But I still could not see the point.

Now, though, there was that poem, 'Hope'. We were asked what each line was about.

'Why did the poet give a watch?'

'He wanted more time.'

'Why did he want more time?'

'He probably wanted to live longer.'

'That's interesting. OK, but why did he give an anchor back?'

A bit of a pause.

'Maybe he was at sea!'

Some laughter. That was too literal. We were beginning to realize that this was not a literal poem.

'What is an anchor?'

'It stops the ship moving.'

'So what is being said?'

'Perhaps he needs something to keep him from moving.'

'Interesting again. Perhaps he is being told that he should be a bit more steady in his life.'

We were beginning to realize that this poem was about life. We did not know poems about life.

'Why does he offer a prayer book next?'

No one was sure.

'Well, I am not surprised you aren't sure about that one. I'm not sure about that either.'

What! The teacher wasn't sure! I had never heard a teacher say he wasn't sure of something. No, tell a lie, we had a wise old RE teacher who would say that sort of thing. But this young teacher – he could actually say he was not sure. That was unheard of.

We were unsettled by this a little. We did not quite know how to react. I would not want to give the impression that it was an instant conversion. We still wanted to catch this new teacher out. He was too cocksure. I remember at the beginning of the next lesson a boy called Trevor Wiltshire put his hand up and asked:

'Sir, what do you do in your crepuscular hours?'

But it did not work.

'Well, I think that would be when I am riding home on my bike.'

Huh, take that you smart arse!

The first lesson proceeded to the end. The bell probably took us by surprise, we were so absorbed in trying to figure out those short poems.

'Right, take out your homework books. The homework is to write a poem and bring it to your next lesson.'

Actually now I think of it I don't think he used the word poem. I think he called it creative writing. Each new thought had to begin on a new line.

'What's the title, sir?'

'Oh, any title you like.'

Any title we like! Astonishing.

'Well, it's YOUR creative writing, isn't it?'

I walked out of that classroom into a new world. I could be a writer. In fact I wrote something about an aeroplane but I did not use the word aeroplane I talked about 'a silver fish'. I thought that was remarkably clever.

Next lesson we looked at 'Mountain Lion' by D.H. Lawrence and I was hooked on poetry for life. (Gardner 2004)

Creating the right atmosphere

Many people consider discipline to be about control, about keeping order. Good discipline, so the argument goes, is about tight control of a class, everybody behaving well and doing as they are told. In such a scenario the teacher is the puppet-master. Nobody does anything without his or her say.

For proponents of that concept of discipline there is – quite often – no desire for much more from a school: good classroom control leads to school and home work getting done on time and that in turn leads to exams being passed. Schooling is seen as being basically about following the teacher's commands and getting good qualifications. If some extracurricular activities are provided, which broaden the mind and might be 'useful' in later life, well that is a bonus. That traditional view of education existed in Lyward's time and is still found today, though not so strongly.

Greg's story shows that it is just as important to create the right learning atmosphere as it is to have unassailable control of a class. First get the class interested and treat them as persons – with minds of their own. Then, despite itself and any poor past experiences, it becomes on your side where it will remain, especially if you show its members how they can start to learn for themselves.

Greg admitted that his scepticism quickly changed to interest (what were these poems about?), and that he soon realized that he could trust Harcourt. He could trust him to give them worthwhile work. Suddenly Greg found himself writing his first poem. From that new interest he went on to read English at Cambridge where he got a first. He became a teacher who has inspired others with a love of literature.

A whole new world

Another instance of a similar turnaround, also of a whole class, occurs in Horwood's memoir *The Boy with No Shoes* (2004) which is full of remarkable happenings. In the sixth week of the their final year before their O levels Jimmy Rova's lower fifth form in an all-boys' school found themselves facing a new teacher, a Mr Wharton, who had replaced a temporary teacher. They were not expected to do well in their Language and Literature papers nor did they think they had much chance of success.

Mr Wharton – or Warty, as he became known – thought differently. He made it very clear what his expectations and hopes for them were. The story is related through the eyes of Jimmy.

First Mr Wharton turned the taking of the register into a little test for himself – to learn all their names. He accomplished this from memory, much to their amazement. 'Something had happened, something new...Here, in our room of failure, a new master had arrived and with him, we sensed, a whole new world' (p.334).

Then he admitted, 'This is the first lesson I have ever taught anyone, which means...' They all waited and wondered what was to come next. 'Which means that we all have *everything* to gain' (p.334).

Everything to gain?, puzzled Jimmy. 'Whatever it meant, it sounded positive, in fact it felt like the first positive thing any master had ever said to us in all our time at the school' (p.334).

Next Mr Wharton dealt with the prevailing staff view of the form. He had been told that as a class they were 'not very good at English' and that they 'might find O levels "difficult"'. (p.334) He pointed out that large numbers of adults came to England to learn English, and that they paid large sums of money to do so. Compared to them they – his class - were already experts. Now experts could not be failures, could they? An expert in English could not fail his O level, could he? No one had ever told them they were experts in anything. No one had talked to them as equals. They had to agree.

He went on to tell them that O levels were simple. At this they grumbled. 'No one ever said O levels were easy before, sir,' (p.335) said one boy. Wharton concurred. 'People like to make examinations seem difficult but really they are not. Unless you choose to think they are.' (p.336) And he got the class to repeat, 'I am going to pass my O level in English language next year', (p.336) getting them to repeat the words louder and louder until they were shouting them. At this point the deputy head, Captain Flax, a stern disciplinarian and very unsympathetic man, burst in, '*What* is going on?' (p.336).

Wharton stood his ground. He apologized to Flax and added, 'Youthful enthusiasm: why not put it down to that?' (p.336) Then he turned his attention back to the class, thereby signalling that he wanted to continue his lesson. The boys watched this staff encounter very closely and picked up the signal – 'the briefest of looks of intense dislike' (p.336) – that Wharton had little time or respect for the bullying Flax.

However, Wharton was already weaving that interruption into his lesson by suggesting what might be learnt from it. 'Sometimes…discretion is the better part of valour. I suggest it would be unwise to be quite so vocal next time… What do I mean by "discretion is the better part of valour"?' (p.337).

Jimmy knew but hesitated in the silence that followed before suddenly saying, 'Think before you act because you might find it's better not to act at all, er, sir.' Wharton agreed and praised him: 'Well done', before adding that it could have other meanings in other contexts.

For Jimmy that 'Well done' felt like the 'first words of praise' he had received in all his years at Stannick Grammar (p.176). (I will return to bestowing praise in a moment.) But Jimmy traced to that lesson with Wharton the beginning of 'the transformation of our academic lives not only individually – as by some alchemy he made each one of us feel special and full of new possibilities by the end of that first class – but collectively as well' (Horwood 2004, p.208).

We do not often get the chance to see a lesson unfolding which is why I have given such attention to both Gardner's and Horwood's recollections. Both Harcourt and Wharton, and Lyward before them in his pre-Finchden teaching days, made each boy in the class feel special and able to achieve.

But it is not enough to address the one. There is also the need to address the many, the whole class; and all three teachers enabled their class to work well collectively.

Wharton expected success from his class. He reckoned it would begin to happen when one boy found some self-belief. That in turn would spread to another, and so on through the form. But he did not just expect success of some general kind. He saw no reason why they should not as a class do better in their O levels than their peers, and alleged betters, the upper fifth. This crazy man was daring them to excel themselves. For the first time their form was united and they wished to succeed.

> Homework was done, boys participated, set books were read, and Warty put into us the belief that we would succeed. Where Flax commanded by fear, Warty did so by engendering respect, perhaps even love. Where Flax punished, Warty praised. Where Flax frowned, Warty grinned. (Horwood 2004, p.339)

And Rova found that time instead of dragging began to race. Soon after he was helped by Wharton to share – as a result of exploring Hopkins's sonnet 'No worst, there is none' – his own 'grief-stricken desolation' (Horwood 2004, p.341) that had gripped him ever since he had seen two young children drown in the sea and been powerless to help them. The poem and the resulting class conversation about its meaning helped him to realize he was not alone. Through the poem he had recognized his grief and loss as 'a chief/Woe, world-sorrow', and come to understand that sorrow was something we all have to face (Horwood 2004, pp.340–42).

After the lesson Wharton and five of the boys stayed with him, having ushered the others out of the room. They let him talk and cry and admit his fears and loneliness before, one by one, each listener admitted that he too had been in that place of desolation. Jimmy was not alone.

Then, brilliantly, Wharton asked the question, 'How do you get out of it?' (p.343). He answered his own question by suggesting that the mountains you think you have to climb are not real but imaginary: they have been planted in your imagination by other people and they are not so much mountains as 'a succession of simple challenges' (p.343). And he went on to say that the examinations were not difficult and that one did not have to learn much to pass them. To prove this he showed them the slim book of syllabuses for all their O levels, and he told them that revising for exams was easy if one had a method. And the method he advocated was to make a series of cribcards. A cribcard was a small card on which you put a likely exam question on the left-hand side before adding the answer on the right.

That chapter from Horwood is one of the most inspirational I know. It demonstrates that good teaching is not just about getting the class on your side by working with you, their teacher, and each other. A good teacher first conveys that good work is expected from everyone and then has to be able to show *how* it is done. And he or she has always to be ready to address the *pastoral* needs of each member – for instance that which troubled them or stopped them from attending. Lyward preferred to talk about *emotional* needs but what he and Wharton were doing was the same thing. The main difference between their places of work was that at Finchden Lyward had to begin with repairing the damage done to the boys' self-esteem and only move them on to serious study when he judged that they were emotionally ready.

Fear or praise?

Philip Beadle, who was awarded the accolade of secondary teacher of the year in 2004, has argued that there are two main ways of getting a class to behave: 'Fear me!' and 'Love me.' Both require nerve, 'a bit of brass neck', and both requests could be refused by the children (2005, p.10).

He recalled being advised as a new teacher not to smile until Christmas. He tried that approach but only lasted ten minutes before a boy told a joke about David Beckham which got him laughing. Beadle thought that you had to be both very certain of your convictions and under the impression that you were infallible to impose a regime of fear, and you could not show any weakness. 'There's no place for apologies in a punitive teacher's class.'

He preferred to use praise for it is very successful at keeping a class focused and on task, as the quote at the start of this chapter suggests. Why is he so certain that praise works best? Because 'everyone likes praise', and those without it are envious of those getting praised. But, and this was a surprising distinction, the focus of praise should be on work and not behaviour 'since work is what we are there to do, and behaving as a civilized human being is a prerequisite to getting such work done.' He takes it for granted that his pupils know how to behave properly. He is more interested in how to keep them working, and he has found that praise does that best. The occasion does not matter: it can be given publicly or privately. Both are just as effective and 'of equal value.'

He cited the Bill and Ted film *Excellent Adventure* with its message of 'Be excellent to each other…dude' as the tactic to adopt. In fact he believed that we should all practise being excellent to each other, especially if we train student teachers, who, having taken part in such group sessions, would arrive in their classrooms 'fluent in the language of praise'.

For Beadle, joking apart, if we treat people the right way they will respond appropriately. 'If we smile at people, they smile back. If someone makes you feel good, you will be good. And if you've got a bag full of carrots, you'll find you don't actually need the stick.'

He has no time for a zero tolerance approach to discipline. 'Enforcing discipline is not of the same value as allowing young people to locate it in themselves. And tolerance is infinitely more likely to work than its antithesis' (2005, p.10).

What then is discipline?

'Disciple' and 'discipline' come from the same Latin word root, *discere*, which means 'to learn'. A 'disciple' is a 'person who professes to receive instruction from another' or a follower; someone who wants to learn (Brookes 2003, p.425). Socrates and Christ had disciples who were shaped and marked by their styles of teaching. (Many teachers since have been inspired by Socrates and/or Christ without necessarily wanting to create disciples.)

'Discipline' has several strands. One is 'training designed to engender self-control and an ordered way of life'; a second, 'the state of self-control achieved by such training', and a third is that it is a branch of learning. More important for our purposes it is also 'subjection to control; order; severe training; mortification; punishment' (Brookes 2003, p.425).

'To discipline' is to subject another (or oneself) to such control or order; 'to train; to educate; to bring under control; to chastise' (Brookes 2003, p.425).

Talk about discipline can cover a wide range of possible meanings. But usually such talk, for example among parents and the general public, refers to the topic of control, and is about the keeping of good order. But there is also the educational aspect of discipline, which includes training but is much wider than that. Thus there is a huge pendulum swing of meaning within the word 'discipline': from on the one hand tight class control to, on the other, the process of educating.

We need to bear in mind this spectrum of meaning when referring to discipline and to make it clear whether we are referring to its 'control' sense or its educational one. In this chapter I am mainly referring to the control aspect of discipline while suggesting that good teaching includes much more than the ability to keep control. I explore what we mean by 'education' – in its fuller sense – in Chapter 5.

Lyward's concept of discipline

Lyward knew as well as anyone the need for the teacher to be in charge of his class and to be able to control it. He had that sort of class control which parents, pupils and colleagues admire. He could keep very good order, if that was what was required. But for him good control was a foundation, a necessary element of successful teaching, rather than the only goal.

And, like any good teacher, he wanted to provide much more than that for his classes. Based on his and their awareness that they were all members one of another, who ultimately sink or swim together, he wanted them to experience a creative kind of discipline.

So relationships mattered: his with his class, its with him; his with each member of the group and each member's with him. A teacher has to make time enough to balance his relationships so that he relates to the whole class (the many) some of the time and to each boy or girl (the one) at other times. Good relationships stem from trust, sufficient relaxation (nobody learns well when they are tense and fearful) and attentiveness.

Trust in the other person enables a necessary letting go of defences or fears, which in turn allows for both attentiveness and sufficient relaxation (but not a switching off). When we are interested in what is going on and able to put our energy into attending to it, then we tend to forget self and become caught up in what is happening or being studied.

D.H. Lawrence, who was a teacher before he became a writer, somewhere described this forgetting of oneself and meeting with others as being on 'holy ground', that place beyond the teacher and his/her class, where they – teacher and class – can meet, caught up in their common task, experiencing something worthwhile which is outside themselves.

Greg Gardner's recollection of being introduced to Herbert's 'Hope' describes such a moment when Harcourt and his new class met on holy ground.

Lyward was not afraid of momentary impertinence or cheek or misbehaviour. He did not rate temporary misdemeanours as anything more than that – a temporary stepping out of line; possibly a cry for attention or a slip in concentration. They might stem from the giving in to an impulse to show off or to get one's own back on someone. He kept such minor infringements in proportion (see Chapter 1).

Like Harcourt, he encouraged creative responses from his pupils. He knew that an overemphasis on control is very likely to stifle creativity and imagination in a child. Rigid monotonous insistence on pupil obedience and conformity creates nothing better than a dull, dreary and lifeless atmosphere which produces dull children.

David Ogg, a history tutor at New College, Oxford, was alleged to have written this report on twins. Of the first he wrote, 'Duller than his brother.' Of the other, 'Less dull.' Witty as that is, it reflects badly on his style of teaching.

Far from providing a stifling ethos a teacher needs to create a liberating and exciting one, heady and intoxicating, as Greg Gardner found in those poetry lessons; the teacher also needs a willingness to take risks.

The teacher, Her Majesty's Inspector and artist Robin Tanner gave a lecture in 1963 in which he declared:

> I believe in living dangerously. I abominate what is cool or only lukewarm. Let us be 'captives of a vision'. Who is not for me is against me!…
>
> I believe in positivity, in openness, in sharing, in doing, producing, constructing, going forward, too absorbed to be careful of one's reputation, too busy constructing to want to destroy. I believe sometimes in starting afresh, in questioning

our most cherished beliefs and prejudices and then in making a change of emphasis or even direction if need be. I cherish fresh experiment. I believe in never standing still. (Tanner 1989, p.4)

Tanner was speaking about the place of the arts in education. Like him Lyward cherished fresh experiment. Neither he nor his class was allowed to stand still. He allowed his pupils room to manoeuvre within an atmosphere where they felt trusted and also encouraged to try out ideas and theories and also make mistakes. He did not aspire to achieve faultless behaviour. Rather he wanted there to be an atmosphere where mistakes could be made, where failure could lead to deeper learning, and lapses of behaviour and manners could be seen as temporary slips.

Control or permissiveness?

For too long discussion of discipline has been polarized along the lines of control is good, permissiveness is bad. In the former the teacher is applauded for his or her strict grip on a class. In the latter the teacher is caricatured as having lost control and the class members do what they want.

   Lyward certainly never advocated an out-and-out permissive style of teaching or favoured a permissive kind of education. The discipline found at Finchden was an integral part of its promise of hospitality. He abhorred the kind of schooling where pupils were allowed to do what they wanted when they wanted. He refuted firmly that Finchden was like one of those modern schools 'where the children are allowed to swear…and go into lessons when they like' (1942, p.2). Earlier, when introducing himself to the readers of *Home and School*, he had written of Finchden:

> We do not stand for 'freedom' or 'self-expression' because 'freedom' can sometimes be a grievous burden and 'self-expression' mere vomiting. We are concerned with providing security within which release and re-education can come to those who have pulled down the shutters on themselves or bitten society. (1937a, p.186)

It is quite wrong to liken Finchden to Summerhill, for instance. Lyward knew A.S. Neill and respected him but he never wished to organize Finchden on Summerhill's lines. Yet past Summerhill students say that its way of educating worked for them, just as Finchdenians are certain that they received something of inestimable worth. Perhaps we should expect flexibility of approach across schools, a form of discipline which is *appropriate* to the child or young person *according to the emotional stage or phase he or she is in*. Chapter 4 develops that suggestion.

Lyward's writings and talks favoured a teacher's need to be subtle by not belonging to one camp, whether it be the control or permissive one. A teacher's method of control needs to match the nature of the lesson. If a test is being taken, then the class may need to work silently with the teacher creating the appropriate conditions. If there is to be group discussion or pupils are to work in pairs to perform an experiment in a science lesson, then conditions must be more relaxed to allow pupils to talk to one another. But the pupils still have to know who is in charge and what are their limits: what is an acceptable noise level, how long they have to complete the task, what are the safety requirements, and so on.

A sensitive teacher needs to mix control (a firm and loving guiding of the class) with the right amounts of permission given to the students to be proactive in their learning: to find out by trial and error, by seeking and then coming back for help when they are 'lost'. Good discipline, in its wider educational sense, is about creating the conditions in which all present, young people as well as adults, can flourish. One aspect of such flourishing is their being encouraged to ask the questions that matter to them without these questions being ridiculed or rejected – even if they find it is much harder to get satisfactory answers.

Providing time enough

Lyward learnt that emotionally damaged youngsters need enough time, not months but years, together with respite from harmful pressures, in order to reconnect with their childhood and, if necessary, live in it for a further spell until they are ready to move on.

Newcomers to Finchden, he knew, were not emotionally ready for formal lessons. They had experienced too much failure in school lessons. Therefore the kind of discipline Lyward arranged for them, the ethos he created, was a form of hospitality, outlined above in Chapter 2. Providing hospitality included arranging for there to be some control, some limits – enough to make new arrivals feel secure – and even more so to acquire gradually a sense of being unconditionally accepted by others there. Furthermore, it gradually became clear to the rather bemused newcomer, who was not used to the luxury of such freedom from pressure, that things would develop for them at a slow pace – sometimes very slow.

For most of the boys the strict kind of control discipline had failed them. It had driven them into themselves and they had gone backwards, not forwards, and begun to despise themselves. They felt they were failures and could no longer trust adults.

It can take time and suffering to discover the right discipline for others

Lyward, after his own breakdown, discovered that he could relate to these emotionally damaged young people, especially the more difficult and unloved ones, who felt that they had been left on the scrapheap. He pioneered at Finchden Manor a way of giving them time, space and loving support and so enabling them to recover their self-esteem, to start believing that they were loveable and of worth both to themselves and others. And only then, after they had been given enough time and respite, were they ready to rejoin the outside world, re-educated and ready to play their part in it.

This was no mean achievement, as Burn (2003, p.233) acknowledged. Looking back nearly half a century later on his residency at Finchden, he told how Jamie Hamilton had commissioned him to write the book that became *Mr. Lyward's Answer* (1956) and an educational bestseller:

> He [his publisher] had heard of Finchden Manor, a remarkable community at Tenterden in Kent for so-called maladjusted adolescent males whom no ordinary school, state or independent, had been able to cope with. An educational genius, George Lyward had founded it before the war and obtained extraordinarily successful results. I went there, was impressed with him, accepted by him, and spent about eighteen months there

passing as a member of his staff, and a few months more studying his files.

Thorne (2003) was another who visited Finchden often, initially as a teacher seeking help from Lyward over a difficult pupil. To him Finchden was a therapeutic community for adolescent boys, a place of hospitality for those damaged psychologically. They were offered respite during which they had time to draw breath and so have a second chance of growing up. For many Finchden was their last hope. Fortunately the fare on offer, the ethos and hospitable discipline, enabled them to go from despair to hope, from 'self-vilification to mature self-affirmation'.

But time is what we all need, whether we are emotionally stable and feel secure in our relationships, or emotionally scarred and aware that we need help or are adjudged by others to need special support. And time is what all teachers have to work in.

And, paradoxically, while Lyward was busy pioneering in a neglected and underrated field of education, he drew continuously on his mainstream and conventional teaching experience. He realized that what he was doing with rejected boys, mainly from the public schools, was appropriate – when adapted – for teaching in ordinary mainstream schools within a conventional time frame, whether the children were five or sixteen. In his new work at Finchden he found he had uncovered a common core of ways of working with all young children. He became convinced that his ideas and techniques were transferable to the nation's schools, where they would bring equally good results.

He was initially cautious about making this claim in public. In an unfinished dialogue with himself about the consequences of a boy's disobedience he claimed: 'But I am sure that there are many adolescents in schools who need what we give.' (1942, p.12) He was not talking only of small schools, for soon after he wrote, 'But I do feel that the knowledge and the spirit behind our way is necessary to a big school' (p.13).

Eleven years later in a published article he wrote:

> But I suspect that what I have found to be the way for these latter ['emotionally and socially retarded or unstable'] is not

without significance for the so-called normal and those who teach them. (1953, p.122)

In a tribute written after Lyward's death, Gordon Toplis, who had been at Guildables and then Finchden, and who became a lecturer in architecture, recalled Lyward's conviction that his way worked for all.

> George Lyward has always maintained that his approach to education is right in principle for everyone. Emotionally disturbed people are, after all, not a peculiar species of individual. They are just like ourselves, only more so. It must not be forgotten that his method grew from his teaching experience in conventional Public Schools. (1974, p.65)

In 1957 Lyward addressed a Leeds conference of West Riding grammar school headteachers on 'Attitudes and standards in Grammar School teaching'. He began by suggesting that 'We all suffered from too much pressure.' He argued that some relaxing, some time for fun, would make a big difference. 'If teacher and pupils had "let go" together for half an hour on anything at all, it might be worth a whole year's work' (Leeds University Institute of Education 1957, p.573k). He was gently reminding his teaching colleagues and the professors present that a sense of fun accompanies sound learning; that working too hard at a subject, applying the control side of discipline too much, was harmful. He went on to urge that schools needed a 'looseness', flexibility and a being able to sit lightly to serious work from time to time. He was not advocating sloppiness or carelessness but he wished that such a loosening would be applied both to methods of teaching and to the school's communal life.

   In the discussion that followed his talk his ideas were challenged. He was accused of not taking examination results seriously. He replied that he was not suggesting what schools should or should not achieve. They had to find their own answers to such questions. He was advocating 'a more relaxed school atmosphere' (p.573q). There needed to be more 'valuable moments in a child's life when the teacher said "let's do something else now"' (p.573q). It was this giving the children permission to relax that would countermand the over-acquisitive nature of education. What was desirable was education that was creative. 'We were living on credit – not in joy' (p.573q). Our main feelings were of 'fear, guilt, inferiority' (p.573q).

Nor was Lyward the only one making these claims for the transferability of the Finchden way of life, its particular kind of discipline and pastoral care, to ordinary schools large and small. When *Mr. Lyward's Answer* was published in 1956 reviewers and others were suggesting that Lyward's way was needed not just for the so-called disturbed boys. For Cyril Connolly, writing in the *Sunday Times* (1956), the book left him yearning: 'the highest compliment I can pay Mr. Lyward and Mr. Burn is to say that I am sorry I am too old to go to Finchden myself – I believe it would have done a great deal for me.'

Harold Nicolson, another eminent reviewer, praised the 'excellent skill' with which Burn 'reproduces' Finchden's 'atmosphere', and he hoped:

> His book will, I trust, be read and read again by all those who are concerned with eccentric children or adolescents; by education authorities, schoolmasters, parents and Justices of the Peace. The ordinary reader will find much interest and beauty in the book, and will in the end discover that his or her ideas have also been readjusted. (Nicolson 1956)

Burn's reviewers also felt that parents needed to attend to what Lyward had been doing. Another reviewer believed that there were thousands of children needing the Finchden way of life. Fifty years on I do not think the need has lessened: it could well have increased. The government is getting more and more concerned about children who are uncontrollable in class and who are disrupting the education of their contemporaries.

Lyward our contemporary

The claim then, from my side of this conversation about discipline, is that Lyward is our contemporary and friend, a teacher speaking to today's teachers and parents and to those of the future. He has useful tips and techniques to share with all who work in schools and colleges. This applies especially to his concept of discipline, in terms of both what he valued and what he ignored or played down.

Some common trepidations

Any teacher new to his task will have anxieties about her or his skill at keeping order, at controlling a class, so that learning happens. New teachers are as likely as not to be apprehensive about their powers of establishing discipline. Anyone who has not had any doubts about their ability to control a roomful of youngsters is either not attending to their real feelings or unusually blessed and very fortunate.

An equivalent state would be an actor waiting to go on stage before an audience. The vast majority of actors, whether raw or experienced, feel nervous, especially when playing a new role. A high level of adrenaline makes them anxious but also 'keyed up'.

A look at newly qualified teachers' (NQTs) experiences of discipline in the classroom confirms that one of the hardest lessons they have to learn is how to discipline pupils. Haydon (2003) refers to a video made by John Fullman, the training coordinator of Southfields Community College in south London. It shows a teacher greeting her class at the door of her classroom, directing them to their seats and getting the lesson off to an organized start. Next there is a sequence of a second teacher allowing her class to arrive and sit down in a chaotic way. She has forgotten some books and sends a pupil back to get them. There is squabbling over who sits where and much time is lost before the lesson can start.

Both teachers were NQTs and so lacked teaching experience but it was the same class of pupils! With the first teacher the class knew what was expected and who was in charge. They were individually greeted and made welcome, and settled calmly and purposefully in the way that Monsieur Lopez had greeted his children in the film about him. With the second the children were acting as they felt, dictating the manner of their arrival, operating according to their own choices.

The point made by that video is that for a teacher to establish good discipline the first thing he or she needs is 'technique' rather than 'charisma'. There are certain practical ways through which a teacher can settle a class and so help it to work together. In Lyward's language this is the start of the process whereby the children come to acknowledge their membership one of another.

The story of those two lesson starts prompts Haydon to pass on several good tips. Quickly learn the children's names and get their help with the pronunciation. Have a seating plan, which will help with learning their names. Stay calm, even if things go wrong and you start feeling angry, and keep your voice down. Rather than shout, whisper. Children are put off, or puzzled, by such a calming approach. Speaking to them quietly and calmly almost hypnotizes them and invites them to listen – sometimes despite themselves. The way you look at people is important and conveys much. 'A frown is preferable to shouting.'

And then, rather surprisingly, there is this advice: 'Just remember you're an actor.' Most teachers would have considered they were very unlikely to succeed on the stage! But teachers become actors in at least two senses: they are acting as substitute parents, they are replacing the parents for the time being, they are *in loco parentis*. But they also have to be actors in that they must stay calm even if they are feeling very unsure of what to do next, fed up or tired. They have to act by bringing to pass the circumstances or conditions that they want for the children at that time.

Marie Stubbs (2003) would support this need to 'act'. In 2000, having just retired, she was invited to take up a temporary headship at St George's, Maida Vale, in order to enable the school to be taken off special measures. It was a Roman Catholic school made notorious a little while back when its head, Philip Lawrence, was murdered when he went out of the school gates to defend a pupil under attack.

Stubbs related at St George's how she often had to smile her way through an ordeal, acting by pretending to be calm and outwardly optimistic, no matter how testing the situation. She instituted a prizegiving at St George's and the first evening was going very well until it was discovered that the car of one of the guests, a distinguished doctor and good friend to the school, had been broken into. His laptop had been stolen and with it the only copy of the book he was writing.

Outwardly she let things carry on as if nothing untoward had happened. She smiled and behaved normally. But privately she had sent a message to the local policeman who was in the audience asking him to see what he could find out. He went off and before long managed to retrieve the missing things, and the evening finished on a good note.

Haydon also makes it clear that teachers, who can turn to senior or more experienced colleagues for support and advice, feel more relaxed and more able to try new ways of creating good order in their classrooms. In addition most teachers welcome the chance to meet with other teachers, to watch a colleague teach and to reflect on a lesson they or someone else taught. Such conferring and reviewing is an effective way of developing good practice and personal confidence. So a school's network of support for new teachers, such as Fullman's, helps not just the teachers but the children who benefit from the teacher's skill and growing confidence and so are very likely to learn more in their lessons.

Similar points are made by Nixey (2003) in her account of the experiences of an NQT, Peter Northcroft, when teaching classics at Watford Grammar School for Boys. Northcroft reckoned the school had an 'exemplary network' of support for its new staff. He had a staff mentor to whom he could talk and there were meetings, once or twice a week, to advise and listen to the NQTs. The head's door was always open so that Northcroft or anyone else could go and talk to him. When asked about his classes, Northcroft said he established strict boundaries of what was acceptable behaviour and stuck to these.

He also felt that in every lesson he 'put on a performance', that he had to be an actor to bring his teaching to life. He even got a professional actor to dress up as a Greek warrior to show younger pupils how the Greeks used to fight.

To the new teacher or inexperienced teacher's nervousness about keeping order we should add that of senior staff, governors and parents, who can get equally twitchy as soon as they sense or hear that someone cannot keep a class in order.

The local community's perceptions

A wider but related issue is the school's behaviour in and out of school. The general public, the immediate neighbours of the school, the shopkeepers and local people all judge the school on its discipline, perceived or reported or gossiped about. Nothing undermines the confidence of the community in a school so rapidly as the perception that its children do not know how to behave and that its staff can not control them. This perception may or may not be true. It may be based more on hearsay, local gossip, than on fact. It may be based on events from the past, now no longer applicable. Such stories may have an element of deliberate malice in them. But the community's confidence will decline until such gossip is scotched and the latest facts show that the pupils do behave sensibly.

What usually drags down a school's reputation are the observed actions and behaviour of its pupils to and from school, and even as they go about their business in the evenings, at weekends and in the holidays when they 'belong' to their parents and not to the school. If the children muck about, create litter, cycle dangerously, vandalize, get in fights or are rude, thoughtless and inconsiderate to others, then their community is going to be critical and disappointed, and quite soon very dissatisfied. One rapid consequence is that potential new parents will start looking elsewhere.

Marie Stubbs, on first arriving at St George's, quickly found that the St George's pupils' behaviour in school was unsatisfactory. She also soon learnt – from talking to local tradespeople – that its local community had lost faith in it. She and her deputies were determined that the pupils' behaviour in and outside the school had to be transformed. Her account of that, *Ahead of the Class* (2003), is a very inspiring story which could encourage both new and experienced teachers.

Ofsted reports rightly give prominence to the behaviour of the pupils and their attitudes to adults and to learning, and act as a further source of evidence of how the school is perceived.

No one would deny the need for good order in the classroom and about the school. Some schools fail to realize that their pupils are judged by their behaviour to and from school. These same schools also do not help themselves by washing their hands of the matter. Stubbs saw that the reputation of the school was affected by all the contacts the community had with its pupils and realized that any improvements in behaviour in school had to be matched by sensible behaviour to and from school.

One morning soon after she had started at St George's Marie Stubbs was emerging from the Tube when she was accosted by a newspaper vendor, 'Hey, Madame, can you come here a minute?' Stubbs went over to him. 'Madame, if you're the new Headteacher you've got a *big* job. You've really got some problems. The kids round here, they steal from me, they're rude, they spit, they fight in the station.' This was said within earshot of St George's pupils, also on their way to school. Stubbs could only smile and reassure him:

> 'I shall make sure that none of the children in *my* school ever behaves like this.' I say these words loudly, so that the St. George's children clattering up the stairs behind us can hear. 'Good. You think you can change things, Madame?' he answers. 'Then I wish you luck – you need it.' (2003, p.37)

Stubbs was fortunate in that the newspaper vendor told her exactly what he and others objected to. Lyward was well aware what Finchden's neighbours and the shopkeepers in Tenterden thought of his boys, especially when they got into scrapes. Things did go wrong. For instance there were cases of trespassing or damage caused to a barn. But Lyward would ensure that he or a member of staff spoke to the complainant, calling on them where necessary, and that any damage was paid for. Relations between Finchden and the locals were usually good enough and they would let Lyward know if they came across a boy who had run away. He enjoyed inviting them to plays, concerts and parties.

A review in the *Kent Messenger* of Burn's book urged: 'Read this book if you possibly can, especially those of you who live in or around Tenterden and have occasionally thought harshly about Finchden's unusual family' ('Invicta' 1956).

Such a tribute confirms that what was being done at Finchden was being appreciated in the wider community.

Valuing talk

Where trust breaks down and where teachers and other adults find children difficult to look after, one likely cause is the way they have been speaking to children. Our manner of talking to young people can quickly – and without our realizing it – convey the wrong message and so arouse a child's resistance, defensiveness and even defiance, instead of gaining his or her cooperation. The shopkeeper in my opening story missed an opportunity to work together with those local children.

Stubbs always spoke in a positive manner to everybody, adults and children – even when the latter were swearing and being rude or disruptive. She was determined that no one should get away with inappropriate behaviour or talk and she would explain what she, and the school, expected in a positive way.

But if the children were to learn how to speak and behave to each other and the staff, then the way adults talked to each other had to act as a role model.

One afternoon, not long after her conversation with the newspaper vendor, one deputy reported that Year 11 pupils (the 15- to 16-year-olds) had been seen climbing over the school wall and bunking off school. With the help of both deputies she collected the names of the 20 or so who had left school without permission and arranged for them to be brought to her office the next morning. The truants excused themselves:

> ''s not just us. Lots of people do it,' somebody mutters.
>
> 'I don't care how many people have done it before,' I say. 'If you're going to learn, you have to be in school. I'm sending letters home to your parents, and you're all going to catch up with the work you've missed in detention. I am going to prove to you, though, that school can be fun. Got that – FUN.' (Stubbs 2003, p.51)

Stubbs made it clear what she and the school expected: that they had to be in school for their learning to happen and they had their final exams in the summer. Their parents would also know what the school expected. She did not harangue them or lecture them and so run the risk of alienating them further. She did not rubbish them by claiming that they were no good at anything, thereby reducing further their self-esteem and very likely getting their backs up even more. She offered them a firm set of expectations. She gave them a glimpse of what she knew they could do, raising their sights, making them look up and beyond the present 'ticking off'. And slipped in a surprise, a new element.

School could be fun. Studying hard could bring its own reward and pleasure. With that afterthought, which enshrined a passionate belief, she moved the conversation out of its danger level, its 'them' and 'us' context, into a new and unifying possibility. There could be satisfaction in school work! That is similar to Gardner's discovery that writing a poem could be fun. Stubbs was very much hoping that they would let her help them to make sure it was fun (even if it had not been in the past). Things could change, no, *would* change, from that moment – if they worked together. And they did. One result was that Stubbs, her deputies, and the year group arranged a Leavers' Ball the following summer, which - despite the teaching staff's reluctance to get involved – was a triumphant success, as the BBC film of her book in 2005 brought out.

It was the same when Marie Stubbs spoke to a boy or girl on their own. She preferred to have a conversation rather than to lecture. Once when eating lunch with the children in the canteen, she noticed a boy eating a sausage with one hand and wiping his shirt with the other:

> 'Why are you eating with your fingers Darren?'...
> 'These plastic forks ain't clean Miss,' he says lugubriously, shaking his head.
> 'Oh, well let's go and sort that out with Barbara [the supervisor],' I say, doing my best not to smile. 'Because you wouldn't want anyone to think you didn't know how to use one.' (2003, p.87)

As with the truants, she pointed Darren forward, towards the table manners she expected (the cutlery was to be used). He would not want anyone to think he did not know how to use a fork, would he?

It was the same with Lyward, who always allowed time within a conversation to steer things round to what he needed to say or to what he hoped a boy might be ready to say. Lyward would quickly sense the creative possibilities of a situation, want to move things on while keeping them fluid, so that a natural change could occur. Talking with, and alongside, a boy or a group of boys to which other staff might casually attach themselves, was one of his ways of achieving this. In time a boy at Finchden understood what was going on, having learnt enough, and then he in turn could enable others to understand more about the place.

Harold Nicolson (1956) cited the story of Henry Carpenter who was once asked by a retired general what the boys learnt at Finchden. 'We learn to live,' was his reply. That night Burn asked Carpenter what he had meant.

'I meant learning to fit in and at the same time to cope. I accept now. I don't worry about defending myself. My energies can branch out' – he splayed the fingers of both hands – 'instead of all going into one clot' and he indicated a point at the end of one finger. (Nicolson 1956)

Given the traumatic, difficult, and uprooted childhood Carpenter had experienced, and the resulting institutional care he had experienced, this insight and the transformation in his behaviour and attitudes were remarkable. He was indeed learning to live.

And 'the process of learning', according to Professor John Danby, another reviewer of *Mr. Lyward's Answer*, 'is the most blessed one given to man' (1956, p.167).

Language and the significance of the first three years

The value of the way we talk with youngsters was introduced in order to show its central role in enabling an appropriate and reasonably relaxed discipline to exist and in creating good relationships. Finchden was a place that upheld and valued talk and the freedom to talk helped deepen the community's life.

Is the same true for the place of talk in our general learning to live, at home and away from school? Polly Toynbee (2004) was excited by the research of two Americans, Hart and Risley (2003). They argued that a child's use of, and exposure to, language in the home in its first three years could determine its future social class. Toynbee was astonished by the potential influence of adults (mothers especially) in the language development of the young child.

This very thorough study of US children in their first three years had collected – by tape-recording – every word a child would hear or speak in every encounter with its parent or care-giver. All this talk was then analysed. The children were selected from three social groups: welfare families (the poorest), working-class families (the middle group) and professional families (representing the middle class and above).

It will not be a surprise that the researchers found that the children of well-educated (professional) families developed their language skills furthest and fastest. The amount of talk directed to these children of professional parents was significant. By the age of four a professional's child will have had 50 million words addressed to it in comparison with the 30 million addressed to a working-class child and only 12 million to a welfare child. That gives a huge advantage to the professional child.

But that child – and this is a surprise – at three years 'had a bigger vocabulary than the parent of the welfare child' (Toynbee 2004, p.22). And when the way a child was spoken to was measured, it transpired that the professional child at three had had 700,000 encouragements offered it and some 80,000 discouragements. In contrast the welfare child had only received 60,000 encouragements in that time and double that number of discouragements.

The third point that Toynbee made was that when the researchers measured children's language and talk aged nine to ten they were 'awestruck at how well our measures of accomplishments at three predicted language skill at nine to 10' (Hart and Risley 2003). This meant that the children's schooling had added little to their vocabulary. Toynbee concluded that after the age of three 'it was already too late'.

This massive study and 'epic analysis' proves that talk is central to the process of educating a child with the early years being vital. Second, it proves that the way we talk to a child, whether we encourage them and invite them to achieve more – the Harcourt, Lyward, Stubbs and Wharton way – or discourage them by criticizing them and finding fault, will make all the difference. Schooling comes after the crucial language skills, speech interactions and amassing of vocabulary, which should be acquired in the first three years, are in place.

Is there an imparting-of-language role for teachers then? Yes, most certainly. But they do need to be aware of, or try to predict, how much talk and encouraging interactions a child has already received from his or her parent(s) at home, and if necessary be prepared to contribute large amounts of talk to compensate where there has been speech-deprivation.

Toynbee is sure the gap between professional and welfare families need not continue. The right sort of intervention works, but many hours of time and talk need to be provided if the welfare child is to catch up with his or her professional peer. Toynbee's remedy is for the resources to be provided to enable good teachers to work in the best possible nursery centres, working with children from all social groups and not concentrating on only the deprived.

CHAPTER 4

An ABC of growing up

In seed time learn, in harvest teach, in winter enjoy. (William Blake, cited in Keynes 1967)

Our life's journey

Lyward's chief discovery was that he could not teach subjects effectively without taking account of the emotional needs and readiness of the child/young person. He acknowledged this on several occasions:

> I came to healing [to setting up Finchden] after 16 years' study of the art of subject teaching – and from a continual discovery of how far the difficulties which appear to reside in the subject were really a reflection of conflicts and uncertainties, emotional problems in other words, of the student. (1959, p.2)

The difficulties which appeared to reside in the subject, Lyward realized, were really a reflection of the emotional problems the young person was coping with. Knowing this, Lyward decided that he had to protect those at Finchden from harmful pressures and expectations. He had to free them from chronological expectations that they ought to be sitting O or A levels. He had to free them also from the nagging or criticisms that undermined self-esteem, and instead allow them respite (or 'respit' as he pronounced it). Once a young person had been given permission to take time out from formal schooling, to be in respite, he could begin to just be – to exist in a safe and supportive environment in which he could regress to a younger childlike stage in order to find and receive a re-education. Lyward often thought of the true ages of the newcomers to Finchden as being around six or seven.

Once that weaning from the wrong pressures had been allowed to happen – and it could take years – then a boy could resume his studies, gain the qualifications he was now ready for, continue his studies at college or university, and take up employment or train for a career.

All this may sound rather simplistic, even naïve, but it worked, as Prickett testified in his look back on Lyward's life (1974). An anonymous reviewer of Burn's book in the *Times Educational Supplement* (Anon 1956) headed his piece 'Healing and teaching' and ended it with this estimate: 'The boys and girls in this country who are awaiting *Mr. Lyward's Answer* must number hundreds of thousands.'

An emotional ABC

Lyward devised his Finchden way of respite and hospitality out of his own experiences and his reflections on others' emotional journey. He called it an 'ABC of growing up', and he outlined it at the start of an unpublished paper on the sonata form in music! The musical analysis in the paper need not concern us. Written possibly for a talk or for a Finchden reader, it began with the following memorable model of our life journey.

Our lives begin in A, childhood, which is the first stage, just as a sonata begins with the first theme or A. In childhood all aspects of the person are present just as all the pieces of a jigsaw exist in its box but are jumbled up and need joining together to make a picture.

We progress to B, the difficult middle stage, associated with chronological adolescence. During it there is the long and painstaking assembly into C, the third stage. Much of the jigsaw joining happens in this often prolonged B stage.

C is the final stage, the reaching of an integrated whole or state of maturity. Lyward was happy to call it being 'grown up'.

That was his outline. There followed a brief gloss on the three stages. Few people, he thought, are ever fully grown up. Most of us remain in B, the middle stage, where we are uncomfortable and find ourselves shifting around. We feel confused and are confusing to others, and are nostalgic for the childhood that we have not quite left behind.

Those of us who are not fully grown up often mistakenly think we have reached C, become mature people, when in fact we have regressed to A, our childhood stage. That was one of his warnings: that A and C can look and feel alike. The other was that B can be prolonged far into the so-called adult years. Far more people are still going through B than they realize, he warned.

Childhood

Lyward wrote extensively in *Home and School* and elsewhere about childhood and adolescence. The Home and School Council published *Advances in Understanding the Child* (1935) and *Advances in Understanding the Adolescent* (1938), for both of which he wrote articles as well as being a member of the group that drew up study materials. At a later Foundations Conference in 1958, he gave a talk on 'The child himself' which included these thoughts:

> The very small child is full of eagerness. He is a creator not a creature; and when he ceases to feel that he is a creator, the significance of things disappears. Because the child is eager, and little, the visual faculty is of tremendous importance. Children are always being told to <u>think</u>. If shown the right way, they will <u>see</u>. The little child is a 'buzzing, blooming confusion', easily seduced by over-praise, blame or cajolery; and then he ceases to be spontaneous and co-operative. Wordsworth saw in the child 'a mighty prophet, seer blessed'. If we could forget that children are physically immature, but remember that they are human beings in their own right, our whole attitude to education might change. The little child is indebted to those around him, but he doesn't know he is in debt; and adults should be careful about this. Too often they bring home to the child that he is a debtor. This is part of our over-moralization of children. Speaking suggestively is one of the most important things in education. (Lyward 1958b)

Lyward liked to keep his definitions and summaries open and flexible and he was skilled at matching his words to his audience and the occasion. From this introduction to the 'child' we need to note three things: the prevalence of seeing in the child's growth; his or her need for room in which to be spontaneous; and the danger of over-moralizing him or her (not praising but criticizing, offering too many judgements). We are asked to remember that children are human beings, adults in the making. For much of the time they are in debt to those around them but we should not burden the child with reminders about this. And it is far better to suggest a child does something than to tell him or her to do it. Suggesting keeps things flexible, allows choice, does not force the child.

Adolescence

Moving next to B, the middle of his three stages, Lyward likened adolescence to 'a mysterious period':

> What does the adolescent see? He has entered into what is primarily an emotional period. The original child emerges again. There is a recapitulation of early life, a revaluation, a ceasing to feel indebted, a realisation of the joy of creating. (1958b)

Before the surge forward there is recapitulation, a going back and over what has happened, a making sense of one's past. Recapitulation in music stands for the final repetition of the theme in a sonata movement after its development (Schwarz, C. *et al.* 1990). Lyward points out some of the novelties of being an adolescent and some of the emotional changes the adolescent is going through (such as realizing the joy of creating); he also points out that the original child emerges again. There will be recapitulation, revaluations, in our living.

Lyward continued his exposition of adolescence:

> The adolescent seeks the adult's blessing prior to experiences which could compel him to acknowledge the adult as a person. He rarely asks directly because he needs to save his face. Thrown, exulting, into the melting-pot he is now excited and pained by 'differences' and a half-felt weakness. (1958b)

In this melting-pot stage differences and a sense of weaknesses and limitations can be bewildering and confusing.

> As an infant he was in the grip of powerful emotional and social forces and his open acknowledgements spelt security. He was indebted to the adult unconsciously – we hope. Now he is being called to attention after shared experiences have partially prepared him to be carried along by those same forces to that which is other than himself. (1958b)

That which is other than ourselves is not only something outside us and different to us but it is also potentially a mystery. The adolescent starts coming to terms with the possibility of mystery and the Mystery, the spiritual–religious side of life. One way of doing that, Lyward suggested, is by thought, which he likened to a 'new power'.

> So here is a person who will use his new power of thought for two purposes, to organize and control his 'external' world and to delay his final exposure to the mysterious inner world at once inevitable, unifying, alluring, threatening. He sees through this and that, but how truly can he be expected to see or see into and create? (1958b)

'Seeing into' leads to understanding – the 'Ah! I've got it!' moments. 'Seeing through' moments are, for instance, when the young person realizes his father or teacher is mortal, does not know everything, is vulnerable, has feelings, is human also.

In Alan Bennett's play *The History Boys* Hector, a brilliant and unconventional teacher, who believes that exams are an enemy of education, unexpectedly tells his sixth form general studies class to get on with their reading. Normally he debates with them, invites them to take part in various verbal games, during which poetry is often quoted and much fun is had, and much unforced learning takes place. But on this day he puts his head on his hands which are on his desk and is silent. Then the boys realize he is crying. They are forced to consider his vulnerability. They do not know what to do or say. Yet they want to do something. Eventually one of them goes up to Hector, pats him awkwardly on the back and says, 'Sir'. The boys have been brought face to face with Hector's vulnerability, his mortality.

'Seeing through' also includes the realization that others say one thing, such as when they tell one how to live, and then do another. It is the discovery of hypocrisy and double standards. Through this mine-field of home truths and unwelcome disturbances and discoveries the adolescent needs his hand held – even if only metaphorically.

> He needs the adult's blessing even while he is re-acting, arguing, being unpunctual, and herding or isolating himself in a condition of moody unfocussed idealism as if for rebellion. Reacting blindly to him is futile, but we can often quietly

include him in such creative responses as we ourselves are able
to make, and so help him to realize that we are, as individuals,
'members one of another'. (Lyward 1958b)

Along with reacting (responding to something, changing one's mind
or repeating some action), arguing, being unpunctual, going around
with a group or isolating him- or herself, Lyward could have included
the adolescent's proneness to be untidy and to live amidst a mess! A
blind or unthought-out reaction from us, our swift criticism or con-
demnation of such behaviour, does not help the young person or the
situation. Lyward insists that 'the child's life must be full of mistakes'.
Yet parents and teachers 'constantly treat mistakes as crimes.' If that is
true for the child, isn't it even more true of our blind reactions to an
adolescent's mistakes?

Lyward concluded his talk with this compressed advice:

> I want to repeat: it is the seeing that matters. Our teaching is
> linear; children are dominated by the cortex. Our education is
> busily preparing 'highly educated' people who are not capable
> of proceeding to the highest. (1958b)

(The wider aspects of what education is for will be explored in
Chapter 5.)

Here once again Lyward is emphasizing the importance of seeing
rather than thinking. He was unhappy about the way most subjects
and topics were treated linearly; that is, taught as though one topic
leads on to another and that, in turn, brings on a third. He argued that
children learn best in a more round-about way, by being taken
forward and back and allowed to shuttle to and fro. As well as being
taught linearly – and some subjects, such as aspects of the sciences,
need that – children should be also taken up and on, round and down
to where they came from. Such a journey would be more like getting
into a London Eye pod and viewing that part of London and the
Thames without being too aware that you were moving forward; yet,
when you disembark, you know you have been on a journey and that
your lofty perch enabled you to see a great deal and to make new con-
nections.

Lyward's second rather coded piece of advice was about the
cortex. The cortex is the layer of grey matter on the surface of the

brain. Lyward had a habit of referring to the cortex in his talks and articles: it was his shorthand for the thinking processes within the brain. He was concerned that much of children's learning was cortex-focused. This happened, for instance, every time a child or a class were exhorted by a teacher or their parent to 'Think! Use your brains!'

Lyward also wanted teachers to teach to a child's feelings. How do you teach to the feelings or, in a parent's case, take your child's feelings into account?

For the teacher it means being aware of the child's and class's feelings, as far as it is possible. To press on with the next topic simply because it is on the syllabus and is the next to be covered may be what I as the children's teacher think is required of me. But is the class ready for it? How settled are they, especially after they have been rushing up and down outdoors in their lunch break? Is there some unfinished business that first ought to be addressed?

There are also wider aspects of the class's 'readiness' to be ascertained. Are the children enjoying the course and getting on with their learning willingly? Or is teaching them rather hard work? If so, what can be done to lighten things every now and then, to give them a little London Eye experience or some respite? Whatever the lesson topic we have chosen to teach, we will find the children respond more deeply if they are emotionally ready.

Lyward illustrated this in a talk to students in 1971–2 on the special education course at Redland College. He instanced four 13-year-olds, two girls and two boys, who were close friends but who had fallen out between lesson two and lesson three. 'What can you do in the way of expecting them to attend to the next lesson?' he asked his audience, implying that the quartet's minds would be on their quarrel. 'Very little. If you shout at them what have you done?' And he let them think about that.

People have rows and cease to talk to each other and go on replaying in their minds what has happened, and so are not able to concentrate on the lesson task.

Lyward also gave another example of a youngster being distracted by something that happened outside the classroom. A six-year-old boy was apparently paying attention to the teacher's talk, which was, let us say, about beech trees, when all the time inside himself he was asking, 'Will my coat be knocked off the peg in the cloakroom as it was yesterday?' That worry was, at that time, the boy's main concern.

The teacher's role in the creation of each lesson is to take into account, and work with her charges' emotional readiness (see Ninian 2001). The teacher's other responsibility is to help the children to be in touch with their own feelings, whether up or down; if down, to know how to cope, and if up, how not to get too carried away. Much of this is obvious and often gets classified under 'common sense'. It is something that many teachers do instinctively whenever they take into account the needs of the whole child. Lyward was well aware that some just plough on with what they have decided to teach, regardless of the class's emotional and motivational readiness.

Parents are teachers to their children whether they wish to be or not. But lest that label overburdens them, let them remember that their child or adolescent will act very often because of a prevailing mood or feeling. The young person is unlikely to draw on reason or to conduct a calm analysis of the options in coming to a decision but more likely to act instinctively or impulsively.

Adolescence, Stage B, is 'primarily an emotional period', Lyward observed (1958b). If so, what can parents do? We parents can try to read what emotions our children are prey to. We can try to work out what is their prevailing feeling – and accept it, even if we do not approve of it or do not understand why it is present. We can get alongside our children and help them find a creative response with which to cope with the situation and their feelings about it.

Finding a model to work with

The above is a simple model to work with. Some of Lyward's caveats and cautions, such as the long time spent in Stage B, are just as applicable today as they were in Lyward's time, and may usefully be borne in mind by teachers when considering the emotional development of their charges.

We do not need to follow slavishly any one model of emotional development. We can draw on several. We need to keep asking, 'What is going on within the young person? What are his or her emotional concerns?', and to remember that Lyward wanted us to recognize that adolescence can last much longer than we might expect.

Playing many parts

Shakespeare had the melancholy Jaques musing on how the 'all the world's a stage' and we are 'merely players' on it who play 'many parts' over the seven ages of our lifetime. According to Jaques these seven phases were:

> At first the infant,
> Mewling and puking in the nurse's arms;
> Then, the whining schoolboy, with his satchel
> And shining face, creeping like snail
> Unwillingly to school; and then the lover,
> Sighing like a furnace, with a woeful ballad
> Made to his mistress' eyebrow; then, a soldier,
> Full of strange oaths, and bearded like the pard,
> Jealous in honour, sudden and quick in quarrel,
> Seeking the bubble reputation
> Even in the cannon's mouth; and then, the justice,
> In fair round belly, with good capon lined,
> With eyes severe, and beard of formal cut,
> Full of wise saws and modern instances,
> And so he plays his part; the sixth age shifts
> Into the lean and slippered pantaloon,
> With spectacles on nose and pouch on side,
> His youthful hose, well saved, a world too wide,
> For his shrunk shank, and his big manly voice,
> Turning again toward childish treble, pipes
> And whistles in his sound; last Scene of all,
> That ends this strange eventful history,
> Is second childishness, and mere oblivion,
> Sans teeth, sans eyes, sans taste, sans everything.

> (*As You Like It* II.7.140ff) (Oliver 1968)

There is a wonderful and alarming finality about that last line, a summing up of great old age and a rounding off of the seven-phased cycle. Shakespeare was well aware that in maturity our faculties can drop away as our bodies droop and wither. There is also a tongue-in-cheek bravado and wit. Four hundred years ago there was no recognition of adolescence, although the lover well depicts one aspect of later adolescence!

One dramatic purpose of this speech is to entertain and divert us from the fact that Orlando, the play's hero, has gone off to fetch the aged and worn-out Adam, his mature and loyal servant, who is dying, having played his part on the world's stage.

Any advance on seven?

In a different model, Erikson posited eight ages of man in his examination of the growth of the ego (1969). Four of his stages – the oral sensory, muscular–anal, locomotor–genital and latency – cover Lyward's A or childhood stage. His fifth, puberty and adolescence, equates with Lyward's B. His remaining three were young adulthood, adulthood and maturity which were equivalent to Lyward's C, being grown up.

In addition Erikson emphasized the psychosocial aspects of his eight ages of man, presenting paired dichotomies, contrasts which reflected progress or set backs. Thus for the oral sensory stage the dichotomy of opposing aspects was basic trust versus mistrust. For the next stage, the muscular–anal, it was autonomy versus shame and doubt. In his fifth, puberty and adolescence, Erikson contrasted identity with role confusion; and in his final stage placed ego identity against despair.

Later he added a basic virtue to each stage. The first's was hope, the fifth's fidelity and the last's wisdom. Adam had exhibited much wisdom as he cared for his master Orlando.

In contrast to Lyward and Erikson, Freud limited his description of our stages of development to the years from childhood to puberty for which he postulated four stages: the oral, anal, phallic and genital (1915, 1923).

All such models are attempts to catch what is still illusory, and are likely to remain so. Lyward's model has – for me - the advantages of simplicity and truth to life. It recognizes the emotional ebb and flow, the going forward and then turning back, which happens in most people's lives. It reflected the way he worked and thought, and, because it rings true to my experience of my own growing and that of others whom I've observed as teacher, colleague and parent, I continue to find it useful.

What price maturity?

Apart from those few people who wish to remain eternally young, the Peter Pan syndrome, the rest of us wish to grow up and to become mature persons. Maturity is the goal, then, but it may take us all our lives to get to it, Lyward suggests. Jack Dominion (2003) describes maturity as the cohering of our intellectual, social, cultural, spiritual and emotional sides into one integrated 'system' which enables us to give love to others, to go out to them in trust and affection, and to accept them as they are.

Dominion is a psychiatrist who has specialized in marital break-down. He believes that far too often our leaders, politicians, lawyers, judges and business men and women, for example, are anything but mature. Over many centuries, he argues, the Western world has promoted intellectual growth at the expense of social, spiritual and above all emotional growth. It has encouraged the growth of the cortex at the expense of our feeling side. It has trusted reason and abstract thought, the core elements of the so-called scientific approach, far too much, and neglected to tend (Lyward would say 'nurture') the emotional side. But neglecting the latter can lead to the breakdowns in relationships which Dominion sees as lying at the heart of much *im*maturity.

His cycle of emotional growth is Lywardian in its simplicity. We move from dependence (on our mother especially) to independence (when we act autonomously by making our own decisions) and then, third, to interdependence (when we recognize our need to live as members one of another and choose often to establish a close relation-ship with another).

Hood (2003) describes maturity as a capacity to think calmly and rationally while honouring and being in touch with our feelings as we carry out our social and other responsibilities.

And thinking is what de Bono (cited in Cassidy 2002, p.11) feels our British system of education lacks if children are ultimately to become mature people. Children in schools are taught to find right answers rather than to think critically and widely in and through a subject. It would seem that de Bono is failing to give due weight and attention to the role of the feelings in thinking critically. Cassidy felt that he redressed the balance, however, in a popular TV series, which she did not identify further.

Thorne (2003), who stayed at Finchden on several occasions, re-called Lyward's dislike of linear thinking: of getting to Z by going from X to Y and then on to Z, when really one needs to get to Z by the quickest and best route.

Another way of describing linear thinking is as activity coming from the left-hand side of the brain. Lyward preferred one to draw on the right side of the brain, the more creative and imaginative side, and so find solutions from a 'deeper', below-consciousness, part of the brain. Claxton (1998) fully endorses that approach.

When needing to make an important decision, Lyward practised a 'both ends', both sides of the brain, form of thinking which he might set out on paper in the form of a dialogue as part of a clarifying process. He would look thoroughly at the pros and cons of possible steps, including the conflicting opposites under consideration, and so make sure that he was weighing up possible responses and outcomes. Such a process gave him the knowledge that he had examined the north and south poles of the matter, and the confidence to go forward, knowing he had really entered into and walked round the subject – as one would if examining a sculptural object.

In an editorial for *Home and School* (1950, p.26) he wrote: 'When-ever "two sides of the question" come into apparent conflict it will be found that one is more truly itself when it emerges "out of" the other.'

The conflict for boys who were referred to Lyward for his help was one between their birth age and their emotional development. The boys he agreed to take were all by chronological age Stage Bs but by emotional age they were Stage As. In which case they needed time, the respite and appropriate care, to complete their childhood phase before continuing with their adolescence. His community consisted of boys who had outwardly behaved as 'big' boys and who had in some cases even been rushed towards so-called manhood. But inside they were frightened insecure children. And Thorne (2003, p.26) tells of the rumour that when Lyward was receiving the OBE from the Queen, she had asked him, 'What is Finchden?' To which he had replied, 'A kind of nursery, Ma'am.'

That being so, it would have been entirely inappropriate to enter these boys for secondary age tests and exams, and he was right to create a way of life built on respite – Finchden's unhurried rhythm of four meals a day – with space in between for the boys to do what they wanted.

Teaching subjects through emotional readiness

In a diary extract (September, 1937a, p.135) Lyward recalled a 'dull' boy of 13 who had visited him. This boy was 'brimming over with life' yet he was not succeeding in class. The balance between security and adventure is always 'cropping up', Lyward observed, both in a girl or boy's life and in the way a teacher responds to their needs.

Next he presented a verbatim account of part of his conversation with the boy because it threw 'light upon the relation between a child's emotional condition and his schoolwork' (1937a, p.135). We have here another example of his fondness for dialogue and how he used conversation educationally. The italicized words in round brackets are the boy's under his breath as Lyward imagined them.

Myself: What's a fracture?

Boy: When you've hurt yourself. (*Let's be personal.*)

Myself: What's a fraction?

Boy: Not a whole number. (*That smudges the lot quickly.*)

Myself: Why do the words look rather alike?

Boy: Because they are spelled the same. (*Any fool can see that.*)

Lyward then drew a picture of an orange and a fractured arm. Pointing first to one and then to the other, he asked:

Myself: How would you make an orange look like that?

Boy: You'd have to cut it. (*If only we could do something.*)

Myself: And the arm...?

Boy: You'd have to fracture it. (*That's a quick get-away.*)

Myself: What does fracture mean then?

Boy: It's more or less the same word (*I'm feeling dizzy.*) as injury, isn't it?

Myself: There's nothing you've said yet that's wrong.

Boy: But it's not to the point. (*I can evidently afford to feel.*)

Myself: Finish this: the orange and the arm have both been...

Boy: They've both been cut out. (*Hesitatingly.*)

Myself: You feel that's not right.

Boy: Yes. (*How funny! It feels more important to be wrong than right.*)

Myself: It's got to satisfy you, not me.

Boy: They've both been moved...[*suddenly*] they've both been broken.

(1937a, p.135)

The extract is illuminating both for the way Lyward could teach and also for the way he observed the boy's feelings and encouraged him to connect with them himself. He concluded this account with his own commentary on the teacher or parent's need to make things visible to the child and to allow him to guess or feel his way when exploring.

> His sudden illumination was due to my having imitated the gesture of breaking an orange and his arm. I wonder how often we are ashamed of the fact that seeing comes before thinking. The refusal on the part of the adult to make things visible or in some way sensible to the child goes along with the refusal to let the child guess (or feel) as a way of learning. But how else is exploring to be done? (Lyward 1937a, p.135)

Before the boy went home they jointly drew the following picture:

2

2 + 3

2 + 3 + 3

2 + 3 + 3 + 3

2 + 3 + 3 + 3 + 3

and when Lyward had reached the fifth line, the boy said: 'Oh, that's algebra.'

Lyward then observed:

> I was sad at that because an intelligent child of nine would have enjoyed it *and have seen what was happening and felt an urge to create.* I know, because I have tried it with small children, very slowly and meticulously and before it had been spoiled for them. *They* were not worried and kept tense wondering what I was getting at. They enjoyed it as drawing and they never failed to see what was happening.
>
> I call that breast-feeding: and I have never met anybody who did not need some re-weaning. In weaning, the *order* is breast-bottle, breast-bottle and the *emphasis* is at first on breast. (Lyward 1937a, p.135)

At this time Lyward described his work as being 'chiefly engaged upon re-education'. Whenever a person needs some re-education – and note that he said above that everyone needs some weaning – 'you and I must be willing frequently to take him back to his mother in order to restore his sense of security' (1937a, p.135). And by taking a boy (or girl) back to his or her mother he meant letting them return to Stage A of their emotional development as if they needed more breast-bottle.

In another diary extract he wrote about calling thin, weedy Richard's bluff (Lyward 1938a). Richard had always compensated for his smallness by being ready to fight another boy, especially if the other was bigger. Climbing trees was another way he could compensate for his titchy size. 'He's a game little 'un', others would say of him. Months after his arrival at Finchden he was still an outsider trying to become part of the community. Lyward observed that his courage was born of a great fear: 'I do not count.' Richard felt he did not matter to other people.

Lyward watched Richard and waited, knowing that Richard was not likely to see the truth of this fear until his sense of being securely inside Finchden and of being accepted by the others for what he was, made his acting macho and being physically adept, 'totally unnecessary *as a form of escape*' (Lyward 1938a, pp.256–257). To be healed of his loneliness Richard had to see himself as a fraud. This he duly came to know, and Lyward was aware of it.

Waiting was what Lyward and his staff had to learn to do. Not rushing a boy on; not revealing what their seeing had taught them about a boy's needs but waiting until he was ready to face a truth about himself, and then helping him through that discovery stage.

Learning to wait

In support of this need to wait, of taking the timing from a boy's own timing, Lyward would quote a poem by Richard Church called 'Learning to Wait'. It meant so much to him that he kept a copy in his study.

> Learning to wait consumes my life
> Consumes and feeds as well
> Where I have loved I love in strife
> That love I could not tell
> I saw it vanish into hate
> Because I had not learned to wait.
>
> This I declare because I know
> That where I love again
> I shall not ask the seed to grow
> Nor grind unripened grain
> But silent in my blissful state
> Serve love through having learned to wait.

> All that I grasped at I have lost
> All I relinquished won
> The marriage of two minds at most
> Deceives till all is done
> And love the conqueror yields to fate
> Strong in having learned to wait.

(Richard Church, source unknown)

There are paradoxes to note, Church has learnt. Learning to wait for the emotional knitting and firming within a boy consumes time. But it also feeds us the waiting teacher or adult. To love or care too deeply about helping another can be harmful: 'Where I have loved I love in strife/That love I could not tell': there is a Blakean echo here. The waiting only works if we can let go of the conscious, contrived loving. We have to be alongside the other, waiting, not pushing or altering anything. We best 'serve love', help the other, 'through having learned to wait.' This has a Miltonic ring. His sonnet 'On his Blindness' ends, 'They also serve who only stand and wait' (in Beeching 1936, p.80).

When Church grasped at a goal, longed for a change in someone, he 'lost': that sort of effort did not help. All he 'relinquished', gave up, in some mysterious way 'won': it yielded results. Even 'love the conqueror' has to learn to wait before it knows the outcome. St Paul's conviction, in 1 Corinthians 13, was that love is the greatest gift we can share with others and that it would outlast faith and hope.

Lyward and his staff had to let go, wait, and only then – one day – would they know what their 'love', their unconditional hopes for the other, had enabled someone else to do or become.

Emotional readiness

Lyward's work and writings invite we who teach or look after children to believe in the concept of emotional readiness. Whenever we care for or work with a person it can help them if we are alert for signs of his or her readiness to learn, and try to estimate where he or she is on their ABC journey to maturity. We will not help people if we hurry them on past where they are currently at. But having learned to wait with them by giving them time enough, we may well find they go on to make exciting strides.

Developing a way of seeing

Lyward created for the boys at Finchden a regime which matched their emotional readiness. Together with his staff he developed a way of seeing. This consisted of observing closely and noting, backed where possible by written notes, what a boy was doing and saying during the many casual encounters and happenings of the day.

This sounds like a form of spying but it was not. Done with love, done for the benefit of the other, in answer to his needs, it became a powerful tool to trace and accompany his emotional state. Lyward knew that the damage a boy had suffered through his self-esteem being toppled led to the boy needing months, even occasionally years, before he felt relaxed and open enough to admit that he was fearful or lonely or trying to be someone other than he really was.

This way of seeing is complex but can be learned, and was picked up by his staff, who were highly skilled at it. It can also be learned by teachers today. It is not something that belongs to a bygone age.

CHAPTER 5

Time enough for education

Writing, when properly managed... is but a different name for conversation. (Laurence Stern, cited in Mullan 2005)

A look back and recapitulation

In their Dark Materials debate on the stage of the National Theatre (*Daily Telegraph* 2004, pp.20–21) Philip Pullman and Rowan Williams chose not to be adversarial but to converse. If the organizers or audience had hoped that there would be a mighty clash and some sensational point-scoring between the acknowledged atheist and the Archbishop of Canterbury, both very influential authors, then they were greatly disappointed.

The occasion, lightly chaired, provided some public time for a conversation where each man could explore topics that he wanted to raise. They shared ideas and reactions, found considerable common ground and accepted without fuss or demonstration where they disagreed. To read their dialogue is to experience their coming closer together as a result of it: indeed, there is almost a sense of apology when they disagreed.

I have chosen not to be adversarial in this book but rather to write it as a form of conversation with you. Another strand has been to suggest that we should value highly the place of talk in education. Lyward has been a highly regarded practitioner in this field as in much else. And Burn recalled Lyward's 'oral lightness of touch' which he felt was missing from his writing (1985). His years of conventional teaching and his pioneering and unconventional approach to caring for emotionally damaged and intelligent young boys at Finchden have been outlined (Chapter 1). I have argued that this approach is applicable not just in a special-school setting but in ordinary classrooms and homes; and that the care with which we create a welcoming and inclusive environment, in which learning and growing can happen, will be experienced as a form of hospitality (Chapter 2).

Thus having our teaching room ready for, and adapted to, the needs of the children is also a physical and psychological way of enabling them to know that they matter and that we are all members one of another. Our actions affect the others in our class, for good or bad. A child's self-esteem partly depends on his or her feeling accepted by both the teacher and the class. No child wants to be cast on a classroom desert island.

For relaxed and attentive learning to take place there needs to be a creative form of discipline (Chapter 3) where the teacher exercises sufficient control for the particular activity whilst also enabling there to be fun and spontaneous sharing of discoveries and blockages. An inflexible, authoritarian style of control will generally prove to be too rigid and repressing.

The teacher or parent – let us not forget that so much learning takes place at home! – is advised to give the child the right support, to create the physical and emotional conditions for successful relating and learning (Chapter 4). Lyward's model of the three stages of a person's emotional growth, which he likened to the form of a sonata, is commended for its simplicity and recognition of the advance and retreat – then advance again – pattern of a person's emotional development. Any ignoring of a person's emotional readiness for learning is likely to cause, at the least, psychological harm.

In all this the matter of time has kept coming to our attention. Calendar time, the rhythms and cycle of the school year, do not necessarily concur with a child's emotional readiness, his or her body and feeling time. Lyward's contribution to our understanding of time has been to urge us to stop the clock for a particular person (or even for a group) in recognition of his or her need to work through an emotional phase; but also, if necessary, to give that person respite from our expectations, from our criticisms or any harmful pressures. That was clearly possible, and successful, in the Finchden milieu where he could experiment and adapt as much as he wanted to. But how can a teacher create respite for a child in an average-sized primary or secondary class?

There are at least two helpful approaches. The first is to give children as much time as possible to grow through their current emotional phase; to decide to avoid putting any pressure on them for as long as is possible (tests or other school demands permitting). A decision to do this, shared with other staff who need to know about it and with the child's parents, together with one's reasons for it, may well be enough to give the child much of the time he or she needs. (We are not going to find a perfect solution in such a context but should be seeking the best fit possible. Adapting Winnicott [1960], we should seek to provide for the person a 'good enough' amount of time.)

The second tactic is sometimes necessary when one has not been able to do the first step as outlined above. It is to resolve, come what may, that there is *time enough*, bearing in mind his or her whole lifetime, for that child to go through his or her various stages of emotional growing. No matter what is expected of the child in the present, and especially if he or she does poorly in tests or is struggling academically, the teacher and parents' readiness to wait and not expect too much too soon will make a big difference. Our unshakeable belief that he or she can succeed one day will be passed on to the child, who will realize that we are waiting with and for him or her and that there is time enough for success to come.

I do not subscribe to the view that says one only has one chance and opportunity in which to do one's learning, and that is at school. That simply does not square with the huge variations in people's emotional readiness for learning. Second, there have never been better opportunities for continuing our studies after we are of school-leaving age; opportunities for taking the courses we want when we feel ready and for continuing for as long as we wish, including into old age, to be students of what we choose. Indeed such openness, such an un-hurried approach to learning and to continuing our education, can match beautifully our internal clock.

This and the next chapter seek to clarify what we mean by education, what goes on in it and what it is for.

What, then, do I mean by education?

The Pullman–Williams debate suggested that there are currently two broad and opposing views. To these will be added Lyward's response, based on ten years of first-hand experience of teaching boys in stable and successful schools and then 43 years – the Finchden years – of having to wait for change within emotionally damaged boys and young men.

I will add my contribution to this topic (in Chapter 6), having first shown how I made use of Lyward's ideas and practice.

In addition examples of good practice from different walks of education will be cited (Chapter 7) with a continuing attention to, and a fascination with, what constitutes good teaching.

Trusting in conversation

To return to conversation both as a way of learning and as a starting point for this exploration. Pullman and Williams demonstrated that conversation can be an agreeable, gently robust, honest and surprising way of learning (2004, pp.20–21). It can help the conversation to get going if there is a simple agenda, which does not have to be adhered to. However, many of the most stimulating conversations just happen, thus spontaneously reflecting the way much of life is one long, improvisatory response to our circumstances, contacts and opportunities. A good conversation is also more likely to encourage learning – travelling together – than the potential thwack and thrust of debate, where point-scoring is expected.

What then can be said in favour of debating? A classroom debate can be an excellent way of developing talk and getting pupils to think about a contentious or tricky subject. Debating is a way of exploring a subject in depth and not just linearly and with the cortex. Passions often come into play. If so, the debaters come to life, start putting themselves, body and soul, into the argument, in order to sway their audience.

But, with older students especially, unless the conditions and purpose of the debate are carefully established, it can become more competitive than truth-seeking; a forum for egotism, a chance to crush not just the other's arguments but even their person. The Oxford Union debates in the early 1960s seemed, with some exceptions, to be more about establishing a speaker's reputation and future career in the union and much less about discovering and sharing truth.

Lyward was a great encourager of open-ended conversation and a skilled practitioner. This book has tried to show how important he considered casual (i.e. spontaneous) talk to be within Finchden whose way of life was designed to encourage all kinds of talk, especially the informal.

There was also formal talk when special events were laid on, including drama and 'party pieces' (which were one-off performances, less rehearsed, more fluid opportunities for sketches and entertainment). The most formal occasions were when Lyward called a session or special assembly. But even during these, while he would be making a serious point, such as calling the community back to its obligations, he would return things to a lighter, more conversational tone. The bulk of the considerable amount of talking and learning at Finchden happened in informal settings as conversations just sprang up. It is surely possible within other forms of schooling to encourage and build in more opportunities for such informal conversations for all: between pupils, between a teacher and pupil(s), between staff and with parents or visitors.

These Finchden conversations sprang up at any time: at table, in one's room or in the common room, outdoors, during an activity or when wandering around. Two people might start a conversation and others, passing by might join in. By which time those involved might well include several boys, a member of staff, possibly Lyward and/or visitors. The staff would be both taking part and casually monitoring what was being shared, and they would encourage, by light steering, a particular boy or boys to talk about something personal and important. Besides their more serious sides these conversations would provide opportunities for light banter and fun.

Prickett, who worked with Lyward for seven years, skilfully reconstructed Lyward's way of 'interviewing' a boy to find out how he was getting on. Lyward may have adapted it from his experiences in the Harrow clinic when he was recovering from his breakdown and was encouraged to talk about how he felt. It was based on Lyward's 'awareness of the need for time so that the deeper levels of (a boy's) personality could come into play' (Prickett 1974, p.58).

Let us suppose that he wished to talk to a boy about his relationship with his mother. Near the beginning of the interview he would, as it were, announce the subject matter of the interview by some such remark as 'You don't get on very well with your mother, do you Peter?' At this stage a monosyllabic reply was all that could be expected, 'No, Sir.'

Lyward would then drop the subject and a wide ranging discussion might follow (he was never at a loss for something to talk about and his witty comments on current Finchden events were sure of a good reception) for the next hour or so. During this time a small group would have been gathered ('You went out with Jeremy yesterday, didn't you? Would you like to have him in?' A member of staff puts his head round the door to ask a question and, if known to be on good terms with Peter, is invited to stay.) Some chance remark will then cause Lyward to return to the matter in hand. 'That's rather like your relationship with your mother, isn't it Peter? Just like Tom hammering at the goal time after time yesterday and each time hitting the post and getting a rebound! Does your mother do that Jeremy? Does she 'go on' at you, does she nag? What sort of rebound does she get?'

If, at this stage, Peter suddenly chimes in and begins to talk about his mother, the interview will have been an easy one. Most frequently the hatred of his mother is so deeply buried that it cannot reach the surface in so short a time. And so, almost imperceptibly, the conversation is allowed to drift away again, and become general. Another friend may be invited to join the group. And so on. Only when Peter at last (it may be after 3 or 4 hours of moving 'to and fro' and, after a stammering start) lets the flood of his anger burst through, only then can the group concentrate on the matter in hand. From then on Peter will be doing most of the talking. The fact that the group of friends is there to share in this confidence has a twofold significance. Peter has brought his trouble out **into the open**. (It would not have been the same if he had said to George Lyward in a huddle, 'I'll tell you, but you must promise not to tell anyone else'). Secondly, it means that those who have (at his invitation) shared his confidence, will both know more about him, understand him better and feel a greater intimacy and responsibility for him. Lyward often said that the boys did far more to help each other than he could do to help them by private interviews. (Prickett 1974, pp.58–9)

The need for time – that was at the heart of Lyward's approach. Granted that the talk outlined above emerged from an interview begun in Lyward's study, it was still informal and wide ranging, and conversational. People were invited to join in and Peter was given time to talk about his mother when he was ready. But Lyward created the conditions for that breakthrough moment when Peter could admit how much he hated his mother. And it was shared with a group of people, made up largely of boys, and those boys were aware of Peter's feelings and would feel committed to looking after him. The boys became healers too.

Clearly in a mainstream school day there would not be such chunks of time for this sort of exploring. But for emotionally and severely damaged children time is needed to let the deeper levels of their personality express their fears or hatreds. Many children in our care in ordinary schools are not likely to be so damaged as Peter or the others at Finchden but they will have worries, fears and concerns. The process that Prickett describes can still be offered them and where possible their peers can be involved, for the reasons that Prickett gives. And we who try to help them need to remember to wait for a young-ster's true feelings to emerge, to allow that it will take time. Prickett again:

> It will be recognized that this technique is time-demanding and exhausting. There is only one thing to be said for it: it works. (1974, p.59)

Being creative with time

Finchden operated on one key principle: that time would be found for each boy's emotional growth to happen where it had been blocked or suffered harm, and in the process he would experience a 're-educa-tion'. Unlike at home or at school, where parents or teachers might be in a hurry for results, it was recognized at Finchden that there had to be time enough to suit each boy's needs.

And by removing any harmful pressures, such as those of school-work deadlines, and by not allowing anyone to be nagged, Lyward immediately created the sense that there was more time than was first thought!

So the boys got up each day knowing that there was, among other things, time for dawdling, time to just be, and time enough for conversational exploring, and so for the gaining of knowledge about oneself and others. Such gains and insights made the world seem a little less hostile, more manageable. There was time for just being – for free-wheeling. One boy, when asked what the boys did all day, replied, 'I don't know what we **do**, but it's a fine place to **be** in' (Prickett 1974, p.56).

No one had to take this subject or that or sit such and such a test because they were in National Curriculum Year 6 or 9, as happens today. There was time for months and years to pass before a boy was judged ready for class lessons. That judgement was based on his emotional readiness and also on his chances of sticking at a course and then succeeding in it.

In the course of resuming his studies a boy would be set questions to answer. He would be unlikely to sit any tests but he would be asked to do some practice questions, to try an old exam paper in readiness for the real thing.

Here then was a completely different and creative attitude to time and to education than is found in our schools. At Finchden time was allowed to exist for each person – for him to grow at his pace, to be shaped by the place, by its hospitality, by its unhurriedness, by the relationships he made, the things he did with others, his community chores, by all the ways he used his time. Time was made to serve Finchden, so far as was possible, and not vice versa.

Time was not there as a kind of authority figure, a means of exercising power or pressure over others. It was seen not so much as a taskmaster but as a friend and ally. Ward began a reflection on the use of time in therapeutic communities with this thought: 'Time is the greatest resource as well as the greatest mystery in treatment...' (2002, p.3). He could have been referring to Finchden specifically. Lyward would certainly concur with the large element of mystery in the way things worked for a particular boy as well as for the community.

In a profound challenge to conventional schooling Abbott (1999) kept pointing out that we underestimate the potential role of other adults other than teachers and parents, who can play a significant part in the wider education of children by giving them time and the benefit of their knowledge and experience; and he reminded us that only 20 per cent of a person's week between the ages of 5 and 18 is spent in school. Eighty per cent of their time is passed *away* from school.

Towards a working definition of education

It is time to return to the Pullman–Williams conversation, which predictably did get round to education. With passion Pullman outlined two contrasting views of the purpose of education. The first was 'to help a child to grow up and so to compete and face the economic challenges of a global environment in the twenty-first century' (Pullman 2004, p.21). The alternative was to help children 'to see that they are the true heirs and inheritors of the riches – the philosophical, the artistic, the scientific, the literary riches – of the world' (Pullman 2004, p.21).

Pullman surveyed our contemporary assumptions about education and felt that today we were offered a choice between whether we 'believe in setting children's minds ablaze with excitement and passion' or whether we wished their schooling to be 'a matter of filling them with facts and testing on them' (Pullman 2004, p.21).

Williams completely agreed with him that true education consisted in helping children to be the heirs of the various kinds of intellectual and emotional riches, and that education was not just about learning facts and being tested.

At this point in their conversation it became clear that their role was becoming prophetic, that they were speaking for a much wider group of people – the majority of teachers and parents and many other educators in England. There has been for some time a deep divide between, on the one hand, a utilitarian concept of education, as it has been forcefully advocated by successive British governments since 1979, and, on the other, the open-ended, flexible, less goal-driven one supported by Pullman and Williams. Both approaches, it is argued, can be imaginatively and creatively implemented. No one side of the argument should try to claim a monopoly of imagination or creativity. The second approach is less driven by means 'to an end' and allows for the unexpected, for the unfolding of talent, for the flowering of a passion, for the discovery of an unexpected interest and, above all, for the variable and often slow process of our emotional side growing awkwardly and unpredictably towards maturity.

I am certain that Lyward's way of educating, before and at Finchden, would put him today in the Pullman–Williams camp. That is where my head and my heart are too, and the rest of this book will suggest that most of us would prefer to be.

The utilitarian view of education, the one the government appears to back, as hinted at by Pullman, believes that we need to turn our children into good adult citizens who will be responsible and reliable and get employment and so boost the economy. Their souls and mental health, their inner lives and private interests, do matter but they become secondary to the greater needs of the State – and the State's number one god is the economy. Measurable progress is sought throughout a boy's or girl's schooling so that there need be no doubts about his or her capablility - and in order to satisfy the employers' request for an adequately educated workforce. What counts within this educational camp, with its very functional view of compulsory schooling, in which schools are required to provide a plentiful and suitable supply of workers for the State's economy, is whether the 16-year-olds have achieved five Grade C (or better) passes at GCSE. After that government attention is paid to their post-16 achievements, especially their additional qualifications, including NVQs and A levels. One government target is that 50 per cent of school leavers should go on to get a degree. When these students have their degree, they are then labelled as 'properly' educated. They have reached the measurable goal chosen for them.

The alternative view is that good teaching does not just produce good exam results and sufficient qualifications, important and neces- sary as they may be. It is part of a bigger, fluid and individual process, which ignites something within children, and equips them with values and aspirations on which they build for the rest of their lives. The French, having grasped that education can go on throughout a person's life, coined the phrase 'education permanente': continuous and unending education. When 'education' happens well, it injects a passion and curiosity into a person, which encourages him or her to ask questions and to, in Rilke's words, 'Live along some distant day into the answers.'

Now asking questions is an awkward business! In asking questions one may be asking for thought, further or new and different thought. One may be challenging others' cherished assumptions or expectations. Politicians, it is well known, can be fearful of having their assumptions and expectations challenged. (They are always fearful of being voted out.) The questioning of their assumptions can make them very insecure. Traditionally they are brought up to fear that such an activity, if not properly restricted and controlled, can lead to some sort of disruption or rebellion. This in turn leads to the assumption that open education (where anything can be asked and explored) leads to anarchy and threatens the safety of the State. There is usually more fear than substance in such a point of view.

It is not just politicians who fear such open exploration. Parents, teachers, bosses and those serving the general public can all feel their authority and power are being undermined, their secure grip of the status quo is slipping away from them, that some aspect of their control is being taken away.

In a letter to a young man, Rilke counselled that he should be patient with himself, allow time to make things clearer for him, and keep asking questions. And rather than hurrying off to find answers and getting impatient, he should 'try to love the questions themselves' and stay with them.

> You are young, at the beginning of everything, and I would like to, to the best of my knowledge, ask you to have patience towards all that is unsolved in your heart and try to love the questions themselves like locked rooms or like books written in a foreign language.
>
> Don't search now for the answers which cannot be given you because you would not be able to live them. And life is about living everything. Live the questions now. Perhaps then gradually, without noticing it you'll live yourself into the answer. (Rilke 1906, transl. Jennifer Cole)

Rilke's plea is applicable to us. It has a universal truth. If we live or stay with our particular current questions, then gradually and without our noticing it we will live ourselves into the answers.

If we apply this advice to the setting of targets, then Rilke seems to be cautioning us – not so much against setting any targets as on our becoming too dependent on them. Targets set for us without our consent by someone else, such as an external authority, are far less likely to motivate and appeal to us than the ones we choose for ourselves which we can live into achieving. Furthermore, if a teacher is trying to encourage a girl or boy to reach a target, worthy as it might be, then much of the energy expended by both may be going into anticipating reaching some milestone, which in turn draws both away from living in and enjoying the present moment.

To define education as schooling for some future achievement is to start losing contact with our now! That is certainly one weakness, a big fault in the current vogue requiring teachers and schools to give so much time and priority to the future achievement of pupil and institutional targets.

Nature, nurture and nourishing

If nature is the state we would be in without nurture, then nurture is the way a child is brought up – loved, fed, clothed, protected and allowed to grow. Nourishing is a way of doing some of that nurturing.

Real education, Lyward believed, was a nourishing process and a recognition that there was time enough to acquire wisdom as well as knowledge, common sense as well as know-how. This slower, gentler, much less driven kind of education brings imagination and creativity to the forefront. It does not predetermine outcomes other than accepting that there has to be some form of public examinations for pupils at some stage(s) in their school life. It takes each child as he or she is, seeing each as a unique person with special talents and interests. It encourages teachers to nurture that specialness of all children by identifying their potential and strengths and helping them to get over their weaknesses or at least to find ways of compensating for them.

By 'nourishing' Lyward meant feeding a little at a time. Nourishing food is good for a child, providing him or her with the right amount in manageable mouthfuls. Cramming is at best stuffing in, trying to bring about quick learning of what is not yet known; at worst it is force-feeding and which pays little or no attention to a person's readiness and is only focused on enabling a pass to be achieved, a qualification to be gained.

Sometimes a person does need a qualification and to gain it some ruthless force-feeding and short-term measures may be necessary, if only to make possible a greater good, such as the chance to work in a chosen field. But that sort of approach can only be justified as a special measure and must not be seen as a norm.

A spoonful at a time

There is, however, no cramming or hurrying on in nourishing. A spoonful at a time is the nourishing, unhurried way of feeding. 'Spoon-feeding', as it can be described, is often sneered at rather than welcomed. But children grow physically a spoonful at a time. In time they learn to feed themselves by spoonfuls. They are dependent on the next mouthful, whether it is given them or they select it. A spoonful at a time takes time and allows for time.

Such feeding removes any sense of hurry, provided the feeder is not hurrying, and any sense of deadlines. Lyward felt that the only good deadline was a lifeline – a way of enabling a person to continue their growing.

The nourishing at Finchden included asking what was good for each boy: how could he be best protected from what was harmful to him? How could he be pleasantly surprised, how included in the fun?

Allowing for slowness

One significant way in which Lyward both practised this nourishing and demonstrated that it was happening was in the reports he – and sometimes his staff – wrote and sent home monthly to a boy's parents. The reports on 'Robin Taylor', are one such example. Robin had arrived at Finchden in the summer of 1946 just after the community had returned from their enforced wartime evacuation to the Welsh Marches.

Two and a half years later Lyward felt that the staff and he could begin to treat Robin more firmly, to practise some of the 'stern love' which he felt Robin by this time needed. Stern love was a favourite phrase which Lyward used when talking about Finchden. It sounds forbidding, grim, even cruel – as if he ran a Dotheboys Hall and had a Mr Squeers side to his character. That association could not be further from Finchden's reality. What Lyward wanted each boy to learn was that there were limits and times when the necessary and most loving and most shaping response to him was a firm 'No'. This sternness should never be understood as separate or apart from the loving care which expressed it, and which was never soft or wishy-washy. And the timing of that 'No' was a skilled matter. Lyward thought that 'we do practice good timing more than a great many – perhaps most – communities' (1942). Good timing often required the staff to wait for a change to happen within a boy, naturally.

In January 1949 Lyward was away and Michael Fitzgerald wrote to Robin's parents on Lyward's behalf:

> As Robin gains more confidence in himself he is moving into a new phase in which he is quieter and less self-assertive. He is not so critical of others and finds it easier to admit his own faults. Definitely a good month. (Harvey 1991, p.340)

Fitzgerald describes Robin as quieter more relaxed and detached, less self-assertive, less critical of others. A month later Lyward wrote:

> Robin has at last played a football match without showing off – and without avoiding the real impact. He moves along slowly as you know, but he doesn't slip back.
>
> He is, I think, discovering that when one 'wills the end' one must include in it 'willing the means'. (Harvey 1991, p.340)

Lyward records one change: Robin has played in a football match without showing off. That is a small and significant step forward in his development which is slow-moving. Robin is learning that an end cannot be achieved without the necessary steps. In a roundabout way Lyward is describing a nourishing form of educating and reminding Robin's parents that it will take time before Robin moves further forward, that they must allow for slowness and that the slow way in emotional 're-educating' was the sure way.

Not long after Robin went home for the weekend, after which his mother wrote to Lyward to say that it had been a happy time and that she felt Robin had 'cast off a terrific load' (Taylor 1946–1951). Lyward's next report, in March 1949, was longer than usual. He began by commenting on how Robin was relating to others:

> Robin is clearly more trustful of others and of himself. We are
> very pleased to notice the greater relaxation he shows when he
> is in a group. There is less of the same tense anxiety to make his
> presence felt. This naturally has resulted in an improvement in
> his football. He can make a mistake without always setting out
> (more or less unconsciously) to dramatize the situation into 'To
> think that a bit of grass stopped what was going to be the
> perfect shot', or something like that. It also means he can con-
> centrate more satisfactorily and be more 'all there' at any given
> moment. (Harvey 1991, p.341)

The anxiety that crippled Robin and which led to his going to
Finchden was gradually falling away. Finchden's way of life was
allowing Robin respite from previous harmful pressures and this, in
turn, had led to his 'greater relaxation' and to an improvement in his
football where he was better at getting on with the game and able to
give more of himself to the present moment.

Although his huge workload made it hard for Lyward in later
years at Finchden to keep up the monthly report pattern on each boy,
it is clear from the examples above that such a practice was ideal for the
passing on of slow but significant little changes and well fitted
Lyward's nourishing approach to education. Just as Robin was treated
according to his needs with ample allowance made for his peculiari-
ties and idiosyncrasies, so each member of Finchden was given time
and attention – and reported on accordingly. As Prickett concluded
(1974), it was costly but it usually worked.

Robin remained five years at Finchden and left when in his early
twenties. He went on to live a full and satisfying adult life. He married
and had children, and he took and passed the exams he needed to gain
professional qualifications in his chosen career.

The poet Hopkins believed that we each have a special quality
which is central to our uniqueness. He called this uniqueness, this
special facet of our nature, a person's 'this-ness', and referred to it by
the Latin word *haeccitas*. Furthermore he felt that part of our uniqueness is that we each have our own 'ring' or sound (Gardner 1948). We
can each make our own music which is unique to us. It is a parent and
teacher's privilege to help bring about that ring, that special music to
emerge. In those reports on Robin we were privileged to observe how

the staff's gentle nourishing and patience, their allowing for his slowness, was enabling Robin's 'ring' to be heard.

Caught in a clash of cultures

St George's House, Windsor Castle, is a non-political and independent Anglican study centre which seeks to bring experts and interested people together in order to aid the process of reconciliation in disputed areas of public life. After one such residential consultation on current attitudes to English education, the House report said that 'education was castigated as being concerned more with economic and social determination, rather than broader intellectual and social values' (St George's House 2003, p.18). And it noted:

> There is a fundamental clash of educational philosophies, with a profound impact on schools, teachers and most importantly a whole generation of pupils, affecting their subsequent performance at college and university and ultimately in work. (p.18)

There, in a nutshell, is a big thumbs down for the prevailing, imposed 'philosophy' of education, the utilitarian model rather than the nourishing open-ended one.

CHAPTER 6

Implementing
the nourishment

*The content, kind and quality of the education we shall find
possible to give our children in any period must be influenced by
the presuppositions affecting the outlook and climate of that
period. We do not see these, we see things through them. (Roy
Niblett 2001, p.208)*

*A ceaseless inventive bodging is what keeps the world going.
(Richard Mabey 2005, p.222)*

A changed world

When Lyward was born in 1894 Gladstone was prime minister for the
fourth time and Victoria was to reign for a further eight years. A loan
could be obtained at one per cent for the day or one and a half per cent
for the week. In Africa Britain was securing its position and increasing
its empire by helping to end the slave trade on the south-eastern shore
of Lake Nyasa (present-day Malawi) through its representative H.H.
Johnstone and the troops under his command (*The Times* 1894).

When Lyward died, Margaret Thatcher was Secretary of State for
Education and the first 600 Open University degrees had been
awarded. The US Skylab astronauts had splashed down safely after a
record 28 days in space. At sea Clare Francis had just sailed the
Atlantic single-handed. The fifth woman to do so, she accomplished
this in her 32-foot boat in 37 days. In the art world Degas's painting
'Les Blanchisseuses', valued at £250,000, had been stolen during its
air freighting to Zurich (*The Times* 1973).

The DNA code had been unravelled 20 years before and the medical and other advances that had followed from this were astonishing and could not have been anticipated when Lyward was a boy.

Lyward was conscious that the world had changed significantly in his lifetime. The UK had changed too: she had let go of an empire and struggled to find a new role. She was about to enter the Common Market. Since Lyward's death in 1973 there have been even more dramatic changes both to the world and to the UK.

In educational matters, were he alive today, Lyward would learn about the National Curriculum and the endless testing of pupils throughout their schooling. (We are said to be the most tested nation!) He would note the greatly increased number of computers in schools and the growing importance of, and reliance on, information technology (IT). It is likely that he would want to debate with Abbott (1999) and others, who argue that learning through IT has to be central in pupils' lives.

He would soon become aware of the centralizing powers of the Secretary of State, the diminishing powers and knowledge about their schools and buildings of the local education authorities (LEAs), and the confusion caused to parents, pupils and teachers by the many types of secondary school.

Lyward would sense that, among the presuppositions of today – those things which underpin our thinking and are taken for granted – was the government assumption that it had the right to set the educational agenda and to 'call the shots'. He would realize that much of the freedom of schools and teachers to develop their own destiny, which he and his contemporaries had enjoyed, had gone.

In matters of morals he would find the media sex-obsessed (and claiming that they were giving us what we wanted), that we no longer entrust our children with any real confidence to strangers and that we are far less likely to trust adults acting in acknowledged positions of responsibility. A general lack of trust in people and in professions formerly used to being trusted (Moore 2002; O'Neill 2002) might well alarm him. As would a tendency to sue someone or some body when something has gone wrong.

It would be much harder for him to start and keep going a Finchden Manor today. Experimental places of education currently struggle to survive: Summerhill was nearly closed down after an Ofsted inspection. Yet they are always needed. Ironically, though, there are signs that diversity in types of schools is being officially welcomed by the government, which has encouraged a move away from uniformity of provision. The pendulum is beginning to swing back away from a rigid central control of schools to a more relaxed approach to what is taught, examined, and inspected.

Reflecting on experience and sharing it

Lyward was an educationalist who also used his knowledge and experience to be a healer. His main medium was talk. In informal conversations with another person or within small or large groups he developed others' self-knowledge and self-esteem. Within the security and trusting relationships of Finchden he sought to bring about emotional and attitudinal change.

He also encouraged a boy to reflect on his experiences and to use his intelligence to bring about change within himself. One teacher trainer and potter who encouraged her students to reflect on their experiences was Seonaid Robertson.

Robertson once took a party of art students down a Yorkshire mine. The students were so moved by what they were learning underground that they identified strongly with the miners in their underworld. Robertson noticed that they returned to the surface tense and very quiet. During the coach journey back to college their oppression lifted to be replaced by a sense of excitement, a siding with the miners in protest against the complacency and ease of college life. They wanted to shout out to their fellows, 'We have been down a *mine*' (Robertson 1963, p.149).

College dinner was being eaten in the dining room as they arrived. But they were not ready to wash and tidy themselves and join their fellows. They were not ready to 'wash off' their experience. They had to relieve the tension they felt, to make some sort of statement. How? Outside the dining room an idea emerged which all agreed on. But, they insisted, Robertson as their tutor had to go in first.

> Slowly pushing open the door of the elegant dining-room… I led the doubled-up students in a re-enactment of our journey through the mine. In the astonished silence of the diners, who

knew, of course, where we had spent the afternoon, we bent from our stooping walk to a shambling crawl, then dropped on all fours and finally we wound underneath the tables and between their legs in that last agonizing creep through the tunnel which was coalface. We did all this in complete and serious silence. Balanced on the razor edge between the solemn and the ludicrous, we were, in effect, saying to them, 'We have been down a mine; we have dragged ourselves like animals on our bellies along the coalface; we have felt the horror of that moment when pit props begin to creak, and we have come back to you not quite the same people.'... As our journey was almost completed and the file was crawling back towards the door I passed under the High Table, and taking from my dirty dungarees pocket the small piece of coal I had clawed out, I wordlessly put it on the clean white plate in front of our Principal – to whom be all honour that he accepted what had to be done and allowed us to complete our silent progress out of the dining-hall. (Robertson 1963, pp.149–50)

Outside again, amidst the cheerful talking and chattering, Robertson knew the tension had been released, and sent them all off to wash and then eat their dinner. The next morning her group gathered but Robertson, instead of giving them a lecture as expected, invited them to respond to their visit to the mine. She wanted them to reflect on the experience, clarify what they had felt and communicate it. She sent them off separately or in groups to do a painting or make a model or write or create a dance – and to spend the whole day over it. She herself made a huge miner in clay, and in the evening they met and showed each other their work.

Lyward knew Robertson. They both attended the Foundations Conferences run in the 1950s by Roy and Sheila Niblett. These were annual April residential get-togethers of some 40 eminent educationalists, professors, teachers, heads, civil servants and trades unionists. Robertson and Lyward were speakers in 1958. It is likely that Lyward knew of her mine visit either first-hand or through her book, *Rosegarden and Labyrinth* (1963). If so, he would have recognized her students' need to re-enact their experience in dumbshow while retaining an element of playfulness.

On a smaller, more ordinary scale similar serious yet playful responses would happen at Finchden. For instance, there was the morning when lots of boys were arriving late for breakfast and Lyward, instead of grumbling about this, announced that he would give two shillings and six pence to the fifteenth boy to arrive late.

Enacting what I had learnt from Lyward

Lyward claimed that his approach and ideas as worked out in Finchden were transferable. He felt that they could be successfully applied in ordinary schools for children of all ages. Well, could they? I thought they could.

After reading *Mr. Lyward's Answer* (Burn 1956), I wished I had been taught in a Lywardian way and decided to become a teacher who would apply Lyward's ideas. From the start I began to implement what I had learnt from Burn's book.

Lyward's core belief was that we are members one of another. At The Mill, Clymping, I sought to make each of my students know that they mattered and were as important as the next person. There were small classes, for the school was a crammer. But each of the boys was there for one of two reasons: the majority because they had failed in their previous schools either to get the qualifications that they needed or to conform to the school's rules, and the remainder because they had come to England from China or Africa to benefit from a private English education.

My job was to build up each boy's confidence and self-belief by showing that he mattered every bit as much as any other boy there and to give him the necessary skills and knowledge to gain the qualifications he sought. I also made it clear to each class that it was in all our interests that everyone succeeded, and that would happen if we looked after each other.

From The Mill I moved to full-time teaching in traditional schools, first in a long-established boys' public school and then, nine years later, to a new and growing upper comprehensive school in Hertfordshire, the Ward Freman School in Buntingford. By then I was a deputy head teacher who wanted to become a head teacher. After four years I was appointed head of Bishop Fox's School in Taunton which, until then had been a large girls' grammar with a sixth form of

250 but, under a reorganization of secondary schools in Taunton, had to become an 11–16 mixed comprehensive. I retired after 19 years there, having taught for some 23 years in state schools and before that for ten in the private sector.

Lyward's influence travelled with me and I felt as strongly that his methods worked when I went to Bishop Fox's as I had when I took the register on my first day of teaching. What I wanted for Bishop Fox's was that all the girls and boys should know that they mattered and that the school wished them well and wanted them to succeed as much as they could. In Lywardian language the one mattered as much as the many. I had the same wish for the staff, teaching and non-teaching: they each mattered and had their own special contribution to make to the well-being and flourishing of the school. I hoped they would treat the children in the way that I have outlined. I also reckoned that within the staff we would find the necessary skills and experience to complement the gaps and lack of experience that were within each of us. Between us we could look after and lead the school well.

A conversation without conclusion

Let me give an illustration of how I worked, first as a classroom teacher. The link with Lyward will become clear.

Late in 1989 I began to plan how I could help my GCSE class the following spring when I would be away on a short sabbatical. I would be leaving them a few weeks before they sat their English papers. How could I reduce their sense of feeling abandoned? Yes, my replacement would play her part and be there to teach them. But there must be something I could do to make it clear that each of them still mattered to me? Something appropriate yet special?

They were shy, withdrawn, cautious students. Most of them were very quiet, slow readers who read little for pleasure and were shy of participating in oral work. They found the written work difficult and unexciting but they were emerging out of their shells and, one day, maybe some time after they had left school, I was sure they would do well enough.

I decided to write a poem to them. We had read poems and plays, including Priestley's *An Inspector Calls* and *Macbeth*, and I reckoned a poem might surprise them enough to get through some of their well-practised defences. It might even startle and delight. Larkin's 'Born

Yesterday' (1988), a poem dedicated to Sally, the just-born daughter
of Kingsley Amis, was full of achievable wishes and modest hopes. In
the previous June they had had to answer questions on it in their
school exam. This is what Larkin wrote:

> Tightly-folded bud,
> I have wished you something
> None of the others would:
> Not the usual stuff
> About being beautiful,
> Or running off a spring
> Of innocence and love –
> They will all wish you that,
> And should it prove possible,
> Well, you're a lucky girl.
>
> But if it shouldn't, then
> May you be ordinary;
> Have, like other women,
> An average of talents:
> Not ugly, not good-looking,
> Nothing uncustomary
> To pull you off your balance,
> That, unworkable itself,
> Stops all the rest from working.
> In fact, may you be dull –
> If that is what a skilled,
> Vigilant, flexible,
> Unemphasised, enthralled
> Catching of happiness is called.

Here was my inspiration, the trigger for what then happened. In a
relaxed and balanced way Larkin shared his hopes for Sally, preferring
to wish for her to be ordinary and dull as opposed to any of the traditional qualities (such as beauty). An enthralled catching of happiness is
a modest wish but so appropriate. The poem is not particularly poetic,
which maybe is why it was chosen for the exam, being chatty and col-
loquial until it ends with a flourish and rich lift.

My poem would be addressed to the whole form. It would start with a general introduction, and then have a verse about each member. It would be serious, hard-hitting yet light in places, and contain some dreams and plenty of encouraging hopes. It would alternate from the general, making points for them all, to the individual, from the many to the one. I wrote it in stages, called it 'Half-Way Hopes' because the class received it half-way through their final year and dedicated it 'To my Fifth Form English group'.

Part one was a trial run. Had it not been accepted I might have abandoned the idea. I introduced it by telling the class that I was working on a present for them, adding casually, 'I could read to you what I have written so far but you may not want that.' To my delight there was a very firm, 'Oh, yes we do!' from most of them. So I read out the first 15 verses which included advice to ten of the class.

They all listened intently, and when I had finished there was a beam on the faces of those written about, while those who had not yet been addressed wanted to be included in the next part. Here is the opening of 'Half-Way Hopes':

A year ago you sat in your 'tightly folded' buds,
In pairs or alone, communicating
More by silence than by smile.
You trusted very cautiously.

To-day I see you very differently:
    poised, becoming expectant.
There is a confidence and zip
    about you that thrill me.
You have begun to 'gel',
    as they say
Not just as persons,
    for you were each always that,
Though often you cared not to
    give much of 'you' away;
No, I mean as a group,
    as Lyward and Priestley's inspector insisted,
As members one of another.

In the opening I was charting how they had grown and changed. 'Tightly folded' is a quote from Larkin's opening line and describes the one-day-old Sally Amis. I had talked to them briefly about Lyward and linked the inspector of Priestley's play, *An Inspector Calls*, with the biblical concept that we are members one of another. I was hesitant about what I wrote for the first few students. The 'Sally' mentioned was one of the class.

> At this mid-G.C.S.E.-year point,
>   may I wish you, Nicholas,
> Stamina and forcefulness:
>   you have the nicest of natures
> Though still hidden.
>
> For Sally joy – sheer unbounded
>   fun and laughter
> In waterfalls.
> For all of you, especially the tempted,
> Regular attendance.
>
> Karen B. – to your energy and application
>   add rhythm, a feeling for patterns
> And an old-fashioned attention to detail.
>
> Pamela – you have so much to give,
>   such presence: remember that gifts
> Are for sharing. Silent conversation
>   gets us nowhere, and a voice
> Is for using: opera singers had to
>   learn to talk first.

The first four of these little reports pick up the positives, which are not necessarily to do with their English, and also point to what still needs to be done, a trick I had learnt from Lyward's monthly reports on Robin Taylor. The reference to their attendance, which in some cases was unsatisfactory, was slipped in – unexpectedly, casually – at an informal moment, as a seed that needed planting. Lyward was adept at dropping serious points into a lighthearted conversation and leaving them to germinate, as an offering, given without fuss or emphasis, without exhortation or moralizing.

Over the years I had pondered on the way Lyward used conversation, within a group and one-to-one, as a learning tool. In Chapter 5 I quoted Prickett's (1974) reconstruction of a typical Lyward interview with a boy, into which others were absorbed and out of which a series of conversations emerged, to show how he used conversation as a learning and therapeutic tool.

One-to-one conversation lies at the heart of the way we learn. A mother talks to her baby. One day the child talks back. The child's stored up knowledge and feelings are very gradually shared, tried out, maybe poured onto a doll, another person, an astonished yet ready and delighted world. Speech is truly a miracle (as is the act of writing – and all creating). Conversation is that miracle magnified, extended, made with another, become airborne.

Instances of conversation
The talkative father

One person very aware that your child will ultimately thrive from your talking to it was Jonathan Smith (2000). A teacher at Tonbridge School, he resolved to take his young daughter out for walks. He would come home from school, put her in the pram and take her for a long walk, talking all the while. He would tell her about his day and about whatever he thought would be of interest to her. These long uninterrupted narrative accounts offered her by her father of his doings and thoughts were monologues. They were hardly conversations. But to converse one person has to listen and take in. Responding comes with readiness.

Smith's faith in the process was rewarded later when his daughter grew into a challenging debater who startled her father by the force and fluency of her arguments.

Tutoring

Tutoring, a true one-to-one form of teaching, is as much about instances of conversation as of passing on skills and knowledge. I was drawn into considering teaching as a possible career by the delights of the one-to-one tutorials I had experienced at Oxford. The conversation began when I entered my tutor's room, became charged with possible material when I read my weekly essay to him, continued after I had finished and covered many things: from the use of the semi-colon in A.L. Rowse's writings to the tendency of the college's societies to die and then be resurrected a few years later. With one tutor it was a commonplace for him to carry on talking even if he had left the room. Once in the summer he sat in his fireplace and talked from there.

During my final year one tutor asked me what work I hoped to do after leaving college. When I replied that I was not sure, he began suggesting in a roundabout way that he knew of something that I could do. After a while I realized that he had a hidden agenda, that he was inviting me to consider applying for MI5 or MI6. That conversation did not lead further!

What both Lyward at Finchden and my tutors were making possible was for two or more people to speak to each other as equals. In the tutorials the dons knew far more about the subject than I did but they each had created conditions which allowed us to engage in talk which was 'without a conclusion' (Oakeshott 1991, p.490) since even though we broke off to go and do other things, the talk could be resumed at the next tutorial or when it suited us. Lyward's use of conversation was invariably informal and without a conclusion.

Oakeshott, in a stimulating essay, likened conversation to 'an unrehearsed intellectual adventure' (1991, p.490), and he defined education as 'an initiation into the skill and partnership of this conversation in which we learn to recognize the voices' [of others] (pp.490–1), and 'to distinguish the proper occasions of utterance', and in which we acquire the appropriate 'intellectual and moral habits' (p.491).

That is a grand and rather formal concept of conversation but it recognizes that there are times and places for conversation and that participating in it is a skill which is learnt through practice, during the course of which we develop appropriate ways of listening, thinking and responding. We learn to adapt our way of talking to the occasion and the person or persons and we learn how to listen to different people. A tutorial is potentially a fit place for conversation, whereas a formal meeting would usually not be. Finchden's form of hospitality, built round four meals a day, was partly created to provide continual occasions for conversation.

The habits which promote good conversation include a willingness to listen and to join in, a readiness both to follow where another has led and to become a leader or starter oneself, the ability to share and respond honestly and a disposition to be both serious and playful, recognizing that the process may lead nowhere – in terms of results – and yet in time take one anywhere.

Oakeshott stressed that a child's talk starts from the playful and moves to the serious, a direction which parents, playgroup leaders and nursery teachers could enjoyably adopt if they have not already done so.

Zeldin (1998) has also written perceptively about the enormous benefits which stem from a willingness to converse with others, including strangers. Proust had an insatiable interest in the details of other people's lives (de Botton 1997). He would engage strangers in conversation and his questions would draw out their life story.

Continuing the conversation about a poem

To return to 'Half-Way Hopes', my best hopes for my class of 15–16-year-olds: the reference to Pamela's silent conversation was an attempt to encourage her to join in the discussions, the class conversation. She usually opted out. Rereading the individual verses I am astonished at how blunt and bold I was.

For instance, Don't run away from yourself, I told Darren. While Jason, whose work had suddenly 'taken off', was applauded for being 'the clearest advertisement / for the educational value of golf!' I also urged him to talk about his dreams. There followed an enigmatic two-liner verse addressed to everyone:

> At times, only when we are riled
> Do we dig for the concealed within ourselves.

That sprang from noticing that some people only participate fully when they have been strongly aroused or even angered by something. Only then do they discover that they have resources which they never knew they had. At this point I used the poem to explain my tactic of choosing to study poetry with them.

> By introducing you to *Macbeth* –
>   (how quickly some of you took to it:
> it was the first time any of you had asked
>   to go away and read up what you had missed!) –
> And Wilfred Owen's war poems,
>   I was hoping that poetry
> Would never be horribly hard again,
>   though one of you wrote above
> *Born Yesterday,* 'Put ruddy translations'.

A grim hopelessness can result for some pupils from an engagement with poetry. Yet one such reader had given me an unexpected bit of humour through her desperate message. But how rash of me to suggest that they or anyone could thereafter avoid struggling with hard poetry!

Among the things I had learnt from Lyward was the inadvisability of nagging someone. I had to resist the temptation to nag Claire, one of that class, or to put harmful pressure on her when she was not getting her writing done. I had to allow her respite, to accept that – for whatever reason – she was not yet ready to commit herself. If I got cross with her and punished her for not doing her home-work, I might have delayed further the moment when she would join in again, become a full member of the class. So for her I had to indicate what was expected of her and also convey that I had still had high hopes for her.

> High hopes I have for you still,
>   Claire, though months passed
> When you seemed to have left the room.
> You are getting organized now.
> Preparation, of whatever sort, will pay
>   dividends with your writing and talking.
> Find your quiet centre first
>   and work from stillness to activity.

Much teaching is planting, sowing an idea, making a suggestion. For an idea to seed there have to be the right conditions: a sense of space and unhurried time; the feeling that something of importance and worth has been offered one. I hoped that the lines written for Claire might also resonate with others in the class. The same may have happened with the ones written for Pamela.

When the poem was complete I read it to the whole class. Later I gave them each a copy of the whole poem. This was what they wanted. The poem was theirs to use in whatever way they wished – as a short personal message, as a general message of encouragement, as a reminder that they were not forgotten.

They could have been in no doubt about my final wish for them:

> You've none of you, probably
>   had to endure one poem
> As long as this. May 1990
>   find you all faring
> Far better than you dared to expect.

I am not clear how much the poem helped them. No one refused it or left it behind. No one asked me what any of it meant or challenged what I had written about them. They seemed to take it on trust. There was an air of satisfaction, a touch of quiet pride, that they had been treated with collective and individual attention. The many and the one had been reached at some level. Some said they had shown the poem to family and school friends. The experiment appeared to have helped them to walk taller. Their GCSE scores were not noticeably better, so far as I can recall, but nor were they the worse for the gift; and they did have a good supply teacher looking after them.

One chance encounter in June 2005, 16 years after they had been given the poem, indicated that some words that I had written had lasted. I happened to meet Kin, a very quiet Chinese boy, good at graphics. We chatted. Yes, I had taught him for his GCSE, he said, and he reminded me that I had written them a poem; he then recalled six words, the first of the lines that referred to him: 'The enigmatic duo, Alan and Kin'. I was intrigued that the phrase 'enigmatic duo' had lodged in his memory. He and Alan had been inseparable and would talk to each other but seldom to anyone else in the class.

If they felt better about themselves and a little more confident as a result of the poem, then the risk had been worth taking. Teachers are planters as much as they are imparters. We have to learn not to expect quick results. Some times we learn later that something we said or did 'clicked' for another. But usually we have to let go of what we have offered and turn to the next task. I had certainly got an immediate buzz from that sort of conversation which was unlikely to have a conclusion.

Getting alongside the other

For conversation to work the two people participating need to be close enough to each other, not talking across the room. An exception is a phone chat where some distance separates the speakers. Even so they can feel alongside each other, able to speak privately and openly to each other. Much of Lyward's way of educating was to get alongside the other as much as possible. I followed that practice when meeting new parents and their children as well as when giving some extra tuition or helping an unhappy or disruptive youngster.

It is sometimes argued that the teacher loses respect and any possible influence for good if he or she gets too close to the pupil and fails to keep an emotional and physical distance. That is true enough. But respect flows from trust rather than from imposed authority. Such authority has a large element of forcing the other person to be subservient or to do something. Within Lyward's preferred way for educating, imposing one's authority has little of nourishing in it, for it speaks of 'You will do X because I say so'. Yet it may sometimes be necessary to impose quiet, to close down a dangerous situation, for the safety of all, by exerting a personal authority.

Lyward was once sent for by Hopkins, a member of staff, because a dangerous fight had broken out between two strong boys, and the staff could not defuse it. Lyward quickly realized that the boys were getting out of control. He clapped his hands loudly and said, 'If you two go on fighting, you are no longer welcome here!' That did the trick. The boys knew that Lyward meant it: if their unbridled behaviour continued they would be asked to leave Finchden.

Fights at Finchden were rare. Lyward's response to that one was all the more effective for being so unprecedented, clear and disarming; and although it may have appeared easy enough to do, Lyward's intervention drained him emotionally and physically.

I probably did not know that story when I found myself early on in my time as a headmaster facing an unexpected situation. There had been local interest, curious rather than malicious, in ouija boards and we (the staff) had made it clear that they were not to be brought to school and were best left alone. One afternoon I heard that several younger children were being frightened by the use of these boards which had been brought to school. I knew I had to do something. So I decided that we would get the whole school together that afternoon. We packed over a thousand children into the hall – it was our normal practice to assemble Years 7–11 or the sixth form but not everyone at the same time.

I explained to the school community that in my view dabbling with ouija boards was potentially harmful. These boards were not to be brought to school. Anyone doing so would not be welcome at Bishop Fox's.

We dismissed the school and everyone went home. The following day the story of that special assembly was in a national newspaper. But we had no further trouble with ouija boards and the school soon settled down. From what I had read and absorbed of Lyward, I think I had remembered two things: the first was that from time to time he called the community together (there was no practice there of a daily 'assembly') for what he called a 'session' (referred to in Chapter 5); the second was that in the session he made it very clear what he disapproved of.

For me Lyward's influence has been formative, wise and very reliable. His way or approach has not let me down. What was unique about his approach was the combination of psychological understanding he brought to his work with adolescents, the way he 'taught' to their feelings and the very strong relationships he built with those whom he looked after. His conceptual framework of our growing up, his ABC, has already been explained (Chapter 4). I find it a useful yardstick.

I have also picked up many tips about the craft of teaching from others – from colleagues, pupils, friends, books and articles – and to a lesser extent from courses and training days.

Aware of Finchden's practice of letting interviews take as long as was necessary, at Bishop Fox's I used to arrange for us to give our visitors as much time as we felt they needed and we could spare. We had not got the flexibility of Finchden to offer hours for such interviews but still tried to give our visitors as long as they needed. We invited boys and/or girls to take a new pupil round the school and left them on their own to get to know each other. We also included other staff and pupils in the conversations as we showed the parents round.

Again, you might say, 'Well, any good school will do that!' I agree. What I learnt from Lyward was to look out for signs of the emotional age and readiness for school of the person we were interviewing. I will call her Amanda. These then would be the sort of things we wanted to find out. How does Amanda relate to her parents (or parent)? How self-composed is she? Is she ready for the school work we will be giving her? How does she relate to other children and adults? Does she speak when asked a question or do her parents answer for her? What are her interests? What is she good at? (That was always something I spent time exploring because success breeds confidence and more success.) And, most important, what are her particular needs? Do we feel we can help her?

All fairly typical, my devil's advocate whispers in my ear! All right, but now comes my particular debt to Lyward's way. He taught me to take an informal and pragmatic emotional reading of Amanda's readiness for school. Is she emotionally younger than her years? Is she at all withdrawn? If so, why? Is she fearful or confident? Is she relaxed or tense? If tense, why? How can we best put her at her ease? Does she have difficulty in trusting others?

If there were concerns along these lines, then I expect that she would need time to develop emotionally and that her academic progress might well be delayed until she had done further emotional growing. In which case her teachers and any staff who looked after her would have to be alerted. We might also have to drop her parents' expectations down to a more modest level and to encourage them to wait with her and refrain from nagging – that is if they would trust and listen to us.

Most of such watching and waiting and gauging of emotional readiness Lyward and others had written about when he was editing *Home and School*. He had called one such article 'Feeling their way through' (1938c, p.115), arguing that an adolescent is deceptive to both his peers and to the adults around him. That was because although 'there is, roughly speaking, a child's world and an adult world there is not an adolescent's world' (1938c, p.115). The adolescent feels that 'he feels everywhere and nowhere'. Adolescence is a term that 'refers to a middle period of change' and it must be understood and responded to by parents and teachers alike as having all the characteristics of a middle period (1938c, p.115).

Lyward used the magazine to encourage teachers and parents the better to understand children and to work together for their good, and its pages are full of common sense and good advice. The magazine was a way in which he could share his ideas and practice beyond Finchden with parents, teachers and professionals. *Home and School* was his forum for conversation with others and for encouraging some of that transferability of practice, that he believed was often urgently needed.

So with a new girl like Amanda I might have to lower staff and parental current expectations, and counsel that she would need time and our patience but that the waiting would in the end be worthwhile. Equally, on another occasion, I might have to speak up for a boy or girl who, staff had decided was not likely to do well in their class, because I sensed their expectations were not nearly high enough.

Another tricky area of school life has always been dealing with disobedient and disruptive pupils (identified in 2005 as a national concern). Lyward had his own, apparently, unorthodox approach to such boys (1942). He might not take any notice if a boy went off from Finchden without permission. He advocated stern love rather than stern punishment. I have shown that he could quell any troublesome behaviour and that, according to the public's expectations of a teacher, he had good discipline. In fact he wanted to keep relations flexible so that the boys took notice of the adult they were working with and came to realize that what was being offered was for their good, even if it included 'noes' as well as 'yeses'. Ghandi (see the epigraph to

Chapter 3) put it well: a 'no' uttered with conviction is constructive, not cramping, in comparison to a flabby 'yes'.

With our difficult or disruptive boys (or girls) my colleagues and I would try various measures to get the child concerned to behave acceptably and to cooperate with us over his or her attendance and work. But if children continued to get into trouble in school and our sanctions were not working, we would talk with their parents, seeking jointly to find a way out of the downward spiral that had developed. If children continued to defy us, then we tried other measures, including referring them to an educational psychologist. If none of these worked, we were likely, then, to 'exclude' them from school for a few days – to make it clear that there were limits, that they could not go on acting in an antisocial way.

According to George Rickey, Lyward in his history teaching would stress the need for limits. But back in the 1920s he did so by urging them to cultivate a 'terminal facility' – to know how to end an essay or task.

At Bishop Fox's we had shown our limits or boundaries on pupil behaviour. On re-admitting an excluded child, we would seek to make some fresh and positive plan with the agreement and cooperation of the family. If the child still rejected what we had to offer and continued to get into serious trouble, we would then, having involved the LEA, call a round table meeting. This would be attended by the child and the parents, an officer from the LEA, whose job would be to see that the interests of the child and the school's concerns were both taken into account, and two senior staff. At this meeting, if there was no sign of a resolution, I would say to the child, in front of his or her parents, 'We think the time has come for some other provision to be found for you. You do not seem able to take advantage of what we have to offer here. So arrangements will be made for you to continue the next phase of your education elsewhere. We wish you well in what happens next.'

What I learnt from Lyward, and other teachers, was that shouting at and getting angry with a boy or girl rarely helped improve the situation. It usually made things worse. In some cases such an adult reaction was what the young person was seeking. Were someone to get angry, then the pupil had gained a kind of power or victory over us.

Then, second, I learnt that there are limits to what a teacher, and a school, should put up with. Lyward was fond of pointing out that there are, and have to be, limits. Third, I learnt that parting with a pupil need not be the final ignominy: it could lead to a new beginning, even to some much needed success and therefore better overall progress. So I ceased getting cross with the 'expelled' pupil and sought to let him or her leave with some dignity and self-respect. Above all I wanted the pupil, and his or her family, to know that we still respected and liked him or her, and that we believed he or she would succeed somewhere else.

That approach worked. In the 1980s a very disturbed boy, who was adopted, was upsetting his parents at home: they thought he was taking drugs. I advised them on several occasions along these lines. 'You are quite right to be concerned. We support you fully in the sort of guidance you are giving him. But I am pretty certain that if you and he can ride this testing time, when he is pushing his luck with you and us, and if you keep showing that you love him and believe in him, he will eventually come through this phase and start using the heaps of ability that we know he has got. However, I cannot tell you how long you may have to wait for this emotional growing to take place.'

It took several years before they phoned to say he was a reformed character and had got a job, and how glad they were that they had not turned him out of his home. I later met him by chance locally and he told me he was teaching drama in a secondary school and really enjoying it.

On another occasion I was walking home after an evening meeting at school when a tall young man came out of the nearby pub, recognized me and came over to chat. I had last seen him at a disciplinary hearing when I had had to tell him that he must leave us because of his wild behaviour and wrecking effect on others. He had transferred to us after being expelled from another local school, and he had never settled. At his departure I had wished him well. Three years later there he was, breezy and cheerful, making the first move to come and have a chat and looking as if he was much more settled.

I did not think that he was emotionally damaged when he had come to us or when he left us. He could not see the point of going to school. There seemed little parental support for it either. He did not see why he should have to waste his time at school or why he should cooperate with others. He preferred to have his freedom.

One further story, this time about a boy in his final year whom we had excluded, we thought, in a correct and clear way. But it turned out that we had made one serious mistake. We had failed to make it clear to him and his parents that we were not writing him off as a person but merely recognizing that there are limits to what we should endure from him when he was being antisocial.

During his time out of school we suffered a night attack in which several walls were daubed and the names of staff painted on them. It took some weeks to work out what had happened and why. The boy concerned was emotionally much younger than his years. Before being excluded he had received such an 'ear-bashing' from staff, which had included his being told that he was not fit for anything, that his response was to go away, as we had ordered, and find a way of hitting back in self-defence. We had hurt him so he hit back – with paint.

Once I realized how he felt, we were able to show him that he had a good future but there were obligations on his part, especially when he was having to work with others.

The school was usually a happy place, lest you might be thinking otherwise. I have been examining beginnings (the initial visit to school) and some of the sanctions or difficult endings (via permanent exclusion). Those three stories are included to show how difficult things can get when a boy or girl resists the pressures that schools inevitably put on pupils to conform, and to indicate that sometimes the school could have handled things better! They are also told to show how Lyward's way of responding to the emotional needs of a person are transferable in a general way. I do not claim to have any special skills in terms of reading a person's emotional readiness for learning. But I have learnt enough from Lyward's way to know what to look out for and when to lift the pressure.

Our Ofsted inspection reported that 'Bishop Fox's School provides a sound education in an exceptionally caring and harmonious atmosphere. Pupils respond very well to the opportunities offered throughout the school' (Tong 1996). Yes, there were several things that we needed to improve on, including some of our teaching and 'managing'. But that pat on our collective backs for the way we got on and for what we had achieved was a tribute to the contribution of everyone to our communal life. I took this as further evidence that Lyward's ideas had been, and would continue to be, transferable into ordinary schools.

Lyward and managing

Lyward did not talk or write about 'managing' a school. 'Manage' was not in his educational vocabulary. He was far more likely to write about aspects of teaching and ways of interacting with a person or a group.

Since his death, senior staff in schools have become known as 'senior managers' who form a 'management team'. Heads no longer lead a staff team, they 'manage' it. Heads of department are 'team managers' (not to be confused with football managers). Governors are responsible for the way a school is 'managed'. In business 'to manage' is to administrate, to oversee design and marketing, to organize other people's doings (*Chambers English Dictionary*). In Lyward's day a manager was not normally associated with any form of 'hands-on' educating. In the 1970s Bishop Fox's appointed a bursar who paid the bills, supervised the care of the buildings and grounds and looked after the non-teaching staff, all of which freed the head to get on with running the rest of the school's life.

Schools have had to become businesslike in the course of running their own budgets but they are not businesses since their prime concern is the social, emotional, spiritual and intellectual growth of young persons. Schools were not set up to sell things (though some heads feel called to raise as much money as they can out of sales). Their teachers teach and look after children. They are not salesmen or women. During the hours of the school day the teachers act *in loci parentis*, as a surrogate parent. Parents have yet to be called managers of children, thank goodness!

In running Finchden Lyward did not resort to staff meetings. He worked informally and so enabled his colleagues to do so also. The staff would chat over breakfast or drop into the staff room after it. They kept in touch during the day and they looked to Lyward for any directing, and when he was away one of them would take over and substitute for him.

Lyward liked to work with someone. He would buzz through on the phone when he wanted to see one of the staff (Prickett 1959). Summoned in this way, Prickett once went to his study and observed two hours of interviews with boys and other callers before being sent off with the files of three boys which he was expected to read that afternoon. Besides his more intensive one-to-one conversations, Lyward used informal and brief chats to learn how a boy was and to move things along. These brief encounters were also valuable ways of keeping things fluid.

It is not clear whether he wrote notes to people but he certainly made notes about incidents and put these into a boy's file, and expected his staff to do the same. (These then might be included in the next report for his parents.) In his absence the staff certainly made, and filed, notes with which to bring him up to date on his return.

I did not therefore find Lyward a guru for the 'managing' of a comprehensive school for he did not want or need to manage. Charles Handy's books were as much help as anything to me for this aspect of my work, especially *Understanding Schools as Organizations* (Handy and Aitken 1986). However, I often wondered how Finchden was run without formal meetings at all, and found this exercise useful – imagine a secondary school being run without any meetings!

That reminds me that Lyward advocated looking at both ends of the spectrum of possible choices before coming to a decision on a matter. For instance, if a parent asked Lyward if a boy could go on holiday, Lyward would reflect on the pros and cons before agreeing or turning down the request. That process was not unlike the tip a friend passed on to me. 'If you are stuck, turn the problem upside down and look at it from the opposite end. By doing so you may see clearly what has to be done next.'

It is clear that in many ways Lyward was a benevolent dictator, unashamedly so, operating as he saw fit – with the checks on him coming from his interactions with his wife, the boys and their parents, his colleagues, the friends he confided in and, above all, his con-science. When he talked to the staff at Marlborough College about

Finchden, he was asked if he was God there. 'Yes', he said, 'and I have to be! I think we all have to be God, at times' (Dancy 2005).

Lyward had no governors or LEA to keep a close eye on him (though he did have to report to LEAs and other sponsoring bodies on the progress of a boy and, if they were not satisfied, they could have withheld payment of the fees or withdrawn a boy). Because he ran a private establishment he was able to say 'no' to His Majesty's Inspectors if he felt their visit was not needed. In some ways he resembled a chieftain – the boys referred to him as 'Chief' – or a medieval baron. In fact he was a humanitarian with power and influence who was left alone by central government. His precious independence allowed him to be an influential educational pioneer ruling in his Kentish manor house. He used his considerable personal power to make Finchden a safe place for the boys he accepted. He guided them, conjured up money or solutions, conducted affairs as if with his private orchestra, improvised and took risks, much as all artists have to do. He wrote that only a poet could understand Finchden and make sense of it. When he had died someone said that only a poet could have run it!

Even if Lyward could not noticeably help me in my dealings with governors and with Somerset's educational officers, there were aspects of his way of working which I could incorporate or adopt. The background paper I wrote for a new set of governors 'Towards better managing' (Harvey 1991, p.680) bears his hallmark. Wanting to introduce the school to them, I wrote about our strengths and weaknesses, and summarized the reorganization we had undergone in the late 1970s and early 1980s (from a girls' grammar school to becoming an 11–16 mixed comprehensive) before sharing our aims and wishes for each girl and boy. In quoting from it, I add a Lywardian commentary within square brackets. An implicit aim for each girl and boy was:

> that we should provide sufficient challenges for our pupils so that they would grow at their right pace [Lyward wanted this for each boy at Finchden] and also provide sufficient boundaries and constraints [he emphasized the need for limits] to prevent them from being destructive or morally soft [he talked about the need for stern love], irresponsible or undisciplined. In addition we need to give them some sort of physical and emotional security with which they can cope with tensions,

setbacks, private griefs, even tragedies [points I had learnt as I read through two large files on Finchden boys and studied Lyward's reports and letters to parents]. Great art is said to grow out of a creative tension or challenge. The same is true of great educating. No school should provide too comfortable or safe an environment, or be too complacent or satisfied in its attitudes or expectations, for it would then fail to challenge its pupils and staff to achieve…their best [without appearing to, Finchden was always challenging a boy to move on – yet waiting with him when he couldn't].

I hoped that Bishop Fox's would be:

a place where you were praised and encouraged rather than criticized or condemned…it is easy to criticize and find fault [Lyward often wrote this, and said it even more]. But people lose confidence in themselves if over-criticized, or are not praised and acknowledged. They lose confidence in themselves if all they hear is that they are no good [pure Lyward – advice he usually passed on for parents' benefit]. They will take risks, adventure in faith, if made to feel good to think positively and realistically about themselves. (Harvey 1991, p.680)

Lyward was passionately opposed to any labelling of a girl or boy. He regarded labels as masks, and as ways we bind people in.

Labels put you in your place, but the place they put you in is on the periphery. The prodding question is a kind of label, a kind of fixative. Not long ago a visiting doctor said to one of our older boys, 'How long have you been here?' The boy replied, looking him straight in the face: 'How long have you been qualified?' (Lyward 1958a, p.8)

Labelling was likely to do more harm than good, and its presence made it that much harder to build up youngsters. I told our governors that it could become a way of fixing our expectations of pupils' likely achievements and attitudes, and so of imprisoning them within our blinkered expectations. To avoid such affixing of attitudes and expectations, we had long ceased to put new pupils into bands (such as when half of a year group has the same curriculum) and streams (class grouping of pupils judged to have similar abilities in most subjects).

Instead our new children were put into tutor groups for some core subjects and sets (ability groups) for others, where staffing levels permitted.

Then in the same paper, once more borrowing from Lyward, I made an obvious but basic point:

> People...develop at different times and speeds and in various ways, and schools have to be sensitive to interpret what is happening within a child; and also to expect a person's adolescence to consist of various phases [a key Lywardian insight greatly simplified, and lightly included, in the hope it might seed]. (Harvey 1991, p.681)

It was then briefly expanded:

> Bishop Fox's would serve its pupils well...if it started with good hopes and expectations for all its members [this incorporates Lyward's belief in our membership one of another and stresses that it matters how everyone fares], and if its staff could develop the ability to recognize what was going on within an individual or a group and so respond to particular and present needs [and not to deal with more than one symptom or need at a time!] (Harvey 1991, p.681)

That was the gist of my theorizing. Next I observed that even when we were a grammar school for girls there were too many girls who were unhappy and not achieving anything like their potential. I acknowledged that no system of educating is going to work for everyone all the time.

> The Comprehensive approach...does start with the preconception that one wants, and is looking for, success – according to age and aptitudes and readiness – from every child. It tries to be inclusive and not to exclude anyone (unless...they persistently choose to refuse to work with us – and even then patient waiting can usually win them round). The hardest task facing any institution is to differentiate between persons so that each is seen, known and treated as an individual [balancing the needs of the one and the many] and yet for the institution also to create and keep a community, where the whole, the school, is somehow more than the sum of its individuals. This concern for

the individual – 'personal attention' – [very much part of Finchden] is always in tension with the need to run the school as a corporate body [each Finchden boy felt he was part of a community which he continued to identify with in adult life]. Rules are needed [Lyward managed with one: thou shalt not pair off! For everything else he and his staff made rulings] but too many rules can turn a place into a legal quagmire [and stop life being flexible, and the staff from responding to what is important at any one moment]. (Harvey 1991, p.682)

What Bishop Fox's stood for – in terms of the style and substance of our educating – was dealt with next; and the following list, again with comments in square brackets, reflects that section of the paper:

- A concern to get our relationships right [Finchden was pre-eminent at this].

- A determination to achieve excellence, so far as it was attainable, for all, in all aspects of our life, via having great expectations of everyone's potential.

- A love of the arts – music, drama, dance, painting, sculpting and modelling – and a love of literature and the spoken or written word [Finchden was rich in this respect].

- A love of making and designing – of problem-solving in its widest sense [also found at Finchden in many different ways].

- A relish for sports and recreational and outdoor pursuits [likewise, and usually kept informal].

- An interest in making our pupils bilingual so that they can travel and converse with or look after others from other countries (i.e. to continue our exchanges and overseas visits).

- The chance, if possible, for every pupil to stay a few nights away from home with a school party, to gain some 'residential' experience and so grow a little more independent.

- The awareness that all this, and so much more, is happening within a Community Education philosophy and framework.

- The school is seen as a welcoming place with an environment that lifts the spirits and encourages contemplation as well as activity.

(Harvey 1991, pp.682–4)

Once more, there is nothing exceptional about these wishes: they were not original, but they grew from what we had achieved and were the fruit of our thinking and dreaming. Now I would add two more, which I strongly believed but did not express in that paper:

- That everybody can succeed at school in something, even if it is not in the more expected ways.

- That a pupil is likely to succeed provided there is one staff member, at least, who believes in him (or her) and supports him through any bad times.

Much of this package I picked up through the schooling I had experienced and in the schools I worked in. Ward Freman School (now Freman College) and its head Roger Harcourt, in particular, taught me much about the effectiveness of the extracurricular side of school life. Harcourt's teaching of English was recalled by Greg Gardner (Chapter 3). In the next chapter I turn to him and Freman College before introducing some other examples of current or recent good practice, which are well worth sharing and which do, in general and sometimes specifically, connect with Lyward's way.

CHAPTER 7

Wider instances
of successful nourishing

In the nature of things life will always keep one step ahead of the
measurers and managers. (Richard Mabey, 2005)

The annual Freman College Shakespeare play

Every December from 1975 to 2003 Roger Harcourt produced a
Shakespeare play at Freman College, a 13–18-years upper comprehensive in Buntingford, Hertfordshire. He had become its headmaster
in January 1975. (I worked with him as deputy head until my move to
Taunton in 1978.)

For each production he chose actors from all age groups, usually
giving the major parts to boys and girls from the sixth form. In the last
12 years he directed *Hamlet, The Tempest, A Midsummer Night's Dream,*
Romeo and Juliet, Macbeth and *King Lear* from the well-known plays and
Antony and Cleopatra, The Comedy of Errors, Richard III, Much Ado About
Nothing and *Love's Labours Lost* from the less often performed.

In the summer another play was performed, usually directed by a
sixth former. Since 1992 these have included two Chekovs, *The Three*
Sisters and *The Cherry Orchard;* an Ibsen, *The Master Builder; Six Charac-*
ters in Search of an Author by Pirandello; *Blood Wedding* by Lorca; *The*
Suicide by Nikolai Erdman; two Noël Cowards and an Emlyn Williams.
Each year there was a house drama competition when the four houses
each put on a play chosen and directed by one of their members, and
often there was a college musical production and other events. In
addition to its strong drama tradition the college also encouraged
music, sport, outdoor pursuits and a host of other activities.

On 6 December 2002 my wife and I saw their *King Lear* which was performed for the fourth time that week to an audience of 150 people of all ages in the Arden Room, their drama studio. The stage was wide but shallow in depth. Three benches were the only fixtures. The painted backdrop scenery showed woods and some open country under a red and threatening sky. Musicians introduced the story with a fanfare and accompanied the Fool's and Edgar's songs and jingles. In three hours ten minutes' playing time we were treated to a memorable, fast-moving and convincing re-enactment of the folly, tragedy and finally compassionate transformation of Lear.

The principals were assured and confident, while some of the minor characters were as good as the principals. There was always something happening to hold our attention and a good pace was maintained with very prompt exits and entrances. There were delightfully subtle, humorous and imaginative touches. For instance, Lear's knights rode children's wooden rocking horses which could neigh.

But how did the young portray old age? With some difficulty. They usually moved as younger people but they had imagined themselves into their parts and so conveyed true feelings. The slowness and failing powers of old age were reached for rather than attained. Their verse-speaking was better than many professionals and audible even when they spoke softly. The feelings of the moment were easily caught and the sense of the story was well conveyed. The teamwork, the ensemble playing and the attentive stillness of those not speaking, were just right.

We had seen Declan Donellan's company of recently trained young actors play *King Lear* at the Swan in Stratford a few weeks before, and found it fruitful to compare the two productions by young people. The older professionals had a panache and brio to their acting, which we expected, and its effect was the more immediate. The college version was more emotionally satisfying and offered a still centre. The Freman Lear, an 18-year-old, was self-contained and fluent until he finally cracked and broke down, drawing our pity to him. The Stratford Lear from the start was larger than life, wild, grotesque, exuberant, brilliant at fooling when drawn on by his Fool. His unreal nature and over-the-top playing became less convincing once the outside storm came and his inner world collapsed.

'The potential that lies, often unsuspected'

Rex Gibson, the series editor of the Cambridge School Shakespeare and Director of the Shakespeare and Schools Project, saw most of the Harcourt productions.

I have watched Roger Harcourt's Shakespeare productions for almost twenty years, and every one has reminded me that the qualities of an outstanding teacher and an excellent director are very similar. Both are concerned to bring out, through respect, deep understanding and quiet encouragement, the potential that lies, often unsuspected, in every student. Quite simply, I've frequently been astounded at the sheer quality his young actors achieve, whether they are playing principal roles, or minor or even non-speaking ones.

Having seen so many of Roger Harcourt's productions, I sense how, as in any good classroom, each student is valued, their talent developed, and their contribution woven subtly but powerfully into a group performance. Under Roger's guidance, Freman College students co-operate to create a three-hour performance that not only enhances their self-esteem, but which also gives great pleasure to those who see such distinguished results.

I could say much about how Roger honours both Shakespeare and his students in each play that he directs. His handling of large numbers of actors on the tiny Arden stage is remarkable. Scene flows into scene with that seamless dramatic energy that characterized the Elizabethan stage, and which is also the feature of any good modern professional production. Inventive but never intensive stage 'business' enhances dramatic effect, and the quality of speaking is wholly admirable, always concerned with clarity of meaning. When a comprehensive school successfully stages *Love's Labour's Lost*, makes sense of its long-lost humour, and, to the modern ear, its over-wrought language, you know you are in the presence of an extraordinarily gifted teacher and director.

Quite simply, I count it a privilege to have seen so much of Roger Harcourt's Shakespeare work at close quarters. He is a headmaster who has never given up teaching for administration, and yet manages a thriving, visibly flourishing school. He is a teacher who genuinely cares for every student, and who not only possesses that elusive quality Kent saw in Lear's face, 'Authority', but whose untiring example motivates and empowers his students, firing their imaginations, extending their understanding and sympathies. Those heart-warming and inspiring qualities have been evident in each of Roger Harcourt's Shakespeare productions I've been honoured to witness. (Gibson 2002, private memo)

There can hardly be a finer tribute to teenage Shakespeare. Several times the *Times Educational Supplement* sent a reporter to cover the college's prowess in drama and to pay tribute to Roger's role (e.g. autumn 2003). What Harcourt and Lyward shared was a belief in the capabilities of every child and although Harcourt never talked about our being members one of another he understood its truth and sought to put it into practice.

The trademarks of a Harcourt school Shakespeare are thorough rehearsing over many months and therefore hours of hard work for all involved, imaginative storytelling, a flair for providing surprises and pleasurable moments and a patient attention to the verse, unwrapping any ambiguities, recognizing its flights of fancy and yet grounding its meaning so that the story can flow on. His company of players are unselfconscious and relaxed. Transformed by the hours of rehearsing, they enjoy giving the performance of their lives before taking their applause with charming modesty.

The Freman College annual Stratford camp

Besides bringing Shakespeare (and much other scripted drama) to Buntingford, Harcourt also took about 40 school members to a summer camp at Tiddington near Stratford for two weeks each August. During that time the camp party saw all the plays being performed by the Royal Shakespeare Company in their three theatres there and visited other theatres to see additional productions. On the middle Sunday the students would put on a short revue of music and sketches known as 'Party Pieces', and on the second Thursday they performed on the green below the Royal Shakespeare Theatre a cod version of a Shakespeare play currently running at the Royal Shakespeare Theatre. Other acts performed during the hour of 'street theatre' included the singing of madrigals and contemporary songs by a choir drawn from camp members and demonstrations of martial arts. This mix of theatre-going, camping and lighthearted performing made for a vigorous and educative fortnight.

Party Pieces was very similar to the Command Performances that Lyward would ask for, at very short notice, from the Finchden members. There was a well-established Finchden tradition of putting on plays each year. In 1950 *Men in Shadow* was taken on a month's tour which included a London performance watched by its author Mary Hayley Bell and her actor husband John Mills.

Roger ran 28 consecutive Stratford camps for Freman College students from 1977 until his retirement in 2004. The 2005 one was on a reduced scale and mainly for adults. *Culture in a Bog* (1998) was Mary Earl's edition of recollections gleaned from camp members. The culture experienced was almost palpable at times and there was a mini Open University 'style' to the set up. The bog has so far remained metaphorical: but the rain of the first year almost persuaded some of us not to return. Each play was introduced at a 'seminar' or lecture on the morning of the day it was to be seen. At first these talks were given by adults, by Harcourt, by fellow teachers and friends, but in later years the lecturers were as likely to be students at university (not all reading English) or sixth formers.

The feeding of some 60 people with an age range from 80 to 3 was delegated to teams of seven or eight each led by an adult or student. For a day each week the duty team cooked and washed up the three main meals and set out the marquee for the morning seminar. Like Lyward, Harcourt was offering hospitality – mostly outdoors – within a simple framework. The quality of cooking and provisioning was superb.

The morning seminar at 9.30 and the evening meal at 5.30, at which theatre tickets were given out, were compulsory. For the rest of the day people were free to do what they wanted. The rules were minimal and sensibly enforced and, like Lyward, Harcourt preferred to give rulings when necessary.

A seminar lasted about 40 minutes and always took place in the ex-Army marquee which would be packed with benches, chairs, tables and people. It started with some notices for the day which were followed by the reading of a short poem, usually read by Harcourt.

Then came a talk about that night's play which was backed up by a list of the characters and themes and ideas in it, chalked on blackboards or written up on an A1 pad. The students were expected to take notes and to keep a daily diary which included brief reviews of the plays. During the seminar there were always moments of laughter arising from good-humoured banter, often between Harcourt and the students, several of whom attended the camps for many years.

During this corporate fortnight much fun was had while considerable informal learning was taking place, especially through the conversations that went on by day – and night!

Through the years Harcourt was the enabler and willing worker for the good of all. His force of personality made the camps work. He was the chief, the boss, just as Lyward was at Finchden. But the original idea was not his. He adopted it from Colin Silk, who had mentored him when he was a student teacher at Lewes Grammar School. Silk invited Harcourt to join his Lewes summer camp at Stratford for adults. Silk was an inspirational teacher of Shakespeare whom Roger later invited, with his wife Beryl, to come on the Freman camps. But no one persuaded Roger to take on the pre-breakfast run to buy the camp papers, eggs, bacon, tomatoes and mushrooms, then, after the seminar, to do the mid-morning shop for the food chosen by the duty team and finally to be the last person to his tent at night. He chose to make these contributions himself.

Living in close proximity with others, in tents or indoors, is never easy. Carole, a newcomer in 1993, was not looking forward to sleeping in a tent but was relieved when she saw hers and found it 'fairly roomy' (Earl 1998, p.110). She began to think that 'this camp won't be as bad as I first expected' (p.110) until she was reminded about duty days; and, worse still, that she had to help get the evening meal ready. Her lifting spirits were shattered. But once she met the others in the team and had prepared some food she began to enjoy herself. Nevertheless for a fortnight when all sorts of demands, planned and unplanned, are made on one, everyone is at times put to the test.

One such discovery was that the experience of sudden and prolonged exposure to 'Art' or, in Zoë Gardner's case, a play performed in the theatre, can be quite tough. She quoted from Howard Barker's poem 'First Prologue to The Bite of the Night' as evidence of being obliged 'to share a little of her life with actors' when she didn't 'understand art', and of having to sit still and 'to see sad things' when she didn't want to, and having to listen. Furthermore she found herself 'Understanding some things / But not others'. Outside in the street afterwards she thought 'If that's art I think it is hard work / It was beyond me' (p.111). Yet she resolved to go again, somehow honoured by the fact that she had found it hard.

Teachers could be seen to be different out of school, human, unpredictable. They could even disagree or be in the wrong or be stupid, at times. As Zoë also discovered:

> At school the teacher always has one-up on you because they've already read and formed opinions on what they're teaching, whereas at Stratford everyone's in the dark about the production we are going to see in the evening. It is really a very useful experience to hear two adults, whose opinions you respect, disagreeing violently and enthusiastically about art, about what they've seen at the theatre that night. Which is another thing you definitely won't be exposed to at school. (Earl 1998, p.144)

To the question 'what do you learn?' Cormac Alexander replied that he found that communal living was a lot of fun and more of 'a learning experience' (Earl 1998, p.32) than a family holiday because he experienced everything with his own peer group. The camps also 'allowed me to do a bit of growing up whilst also having an excellent time' and, afterwards, when he had to study more Shakespeare plays, 'I realized exactly how much learning was actually packed into those two weeks' (p.32). Greg Gardner, when still at school, learnt from Harcourt that instead of standing on the outskirts of The Winter's Tale thinking that acting was 'the most frightening, appalling thing to ask anybody to do', he could play Brutus in Julius Caesar (p.22).

These spells of living in a tented community can be compared to the Finchden experience that Lyward provided. There were difficulties of relationships, there were demands made on everyone within the communal living, especially when on duty, and when setting up camp or giving a seminar – and yet we accepted that it was Roger's show and that he knew what he was doing.

Most of the adult volunteers, including my wife and I – and our children – have kept on returning. We valued the friendships made and the way we were accepted by the young. We knew that our horizons were continually being extended and that these fortnights by the Avon were a nourishing and satisfying way of continuing to learn. For me the pull of Shakespeare is overpowering.

The PROMISE mentoring scheme

Six years ago an imaginative mentoring scheme called PROMISE was launched in Somerset. It was a multi-agency initiative led by Social Services and funded by Somerset County Council and the government's Single Regeneration Budget. The target group was the most 'at risk' young people in Somerset. A team was set up by Linda Barnett and it was led by Rod Salter and Stella Marshall. Adult volunteers were invited to apply to become mentors, and the first group were trained and placed.

The mentors were asked to visit their teenage boy or girl once a week for two or three hours, and to offer them friendship and any practical help. But why were mentors needed?

Unacceptable behaviour, patchy school attendance, low school achievement, problems with relationships and getting into trouble, such as committing petty crimes, and then being referred to the police or taken to court or adjudged as needing psychiatric help, are some of the reasons why some 500–600 Somerset youngsters were of concern to Social Services. These young people also suffered from low self-esteem and sensed that the world was against them. For those lacking a family or foster home their home has to be a children's one. These 'at risk' often lacked love, especially the warm caring adult sort that holds and supports one but also enables one to laugh and cry at the wonders and vagaries of the world. Often they were not accustomed or encouraged to play enough or to respond playfully. To them life was relentless and grim; a struggle which did not seem to be going anywhere.

It was to change this mindset that Salter and Marshall sought the help of mentors. In naming the project PROMISE did they seek to instil hope where it had been lacking? Maybe. They certainly promised the mentors that they were always available.

Salter and Marshall arranged to be 'on call' 24 hours a day for a mentor to chat with them about any problems. They have kept their promise, and their readiness to help a mentor at any time has been a core element in the success of the scheme. The mentors know that support is available when they need it and take advantage of it.

Similarly Lyward's staff and the boys at Finchden knew that he was there when needed. At any hour of the night and day they could turn to him. Likewise most of the staff made themselves similarly available to the boys.

The PROMISE scheme is proving to be a great success and there are currently more volunteers wishing to become mentors than can be accommodated. I have attended two conferences at which mentors talked about their role and I have got to know several mentors. All speak highly of their training and support, and are enthusiastic about their relationship with their mentees. Independent evaluations of the scheme have confirmed that, and also that the young people benefit enormously, usually gaining greatly in self-confidence, and feel valued by someone outside their immediate circle.

One person's story and experiences can often highlight so much. Here then is an account of how one mentor worked, and what she noticed was happening.

Being ready to walk the extra mile

Tina Herbert read about the PROMISE mentoring scheme in a leaflet and felt she wanted to be part of it. She already had worked with young people and she had two young children. She completed the training and then waited for a placement. She was offered the chance to be Julie's mentor. Rod introduced them, and both Tina and Julie, who was 14, were nervous about what might happen and whether they would get on, but they decided to give it a try.

Over the next 18 months they met once a week for two to three hours, except when Tina was away. During this time Tina realized she had become the one constant person in Julie's life, for Julie had no parents and was brought up by a grandmother who allegedly abused her. At times Julie had self-harmed, so low was her self-esteem, and both these facts were known before Tina's placement was arranged.

Another complicating factor was that Julie moved several times during her mentoring: first to a care home, then to foster parents, then to a specialist unit in Wiltshire, and then into local authority rented accommodation. Wherever she was Tina had visited her, even when that meant a two-hour drive. Their relationship survived these moves: they continued to get on even though the venues changed.

Julie was tall and beautiful and desperately wanted to be loved. Emotionally she was more like a young child. She came to trust Tina and grew very clingy. She would take Tina's arm when they went out, and indoors she might take her handbag and sit on the floor and go through its contents, tidying up as she did so. To Julie Tina was someone who was on her side, whom she could ring at any time – and did! She began coming to Tina's house and she got to know her children who accepted her into their home. When Tina's children were doing jobs for her, she would give Julie one too, such as a chair to paint.

The day came when Julie begged Tina to adopt her. That put Tina on the spot. If she said no, then Julie would feel rejected and unwanted. If she said yes how would that affect her children? Would they feel displaced? After much agonizing, Tina decided she could not adopt Julie and explained why, making it clear that she would carry on visiting and befriending her.

Salter (2005a) and Marshall always make it clear both to the young person and to the mentor of the likely risks of the mentee becoming too dependent on the mentor and of the potential harm this could cause. Salter believes that the young people seem to understand when he stresses that the quality of the relationship – the trust and the natural affection engendered – is likely to suffer if the mentor takes on a different role, such as becoming his or her parent by adopting them. It was that warning of Salter's that may have further contributed to Tina's deciding against adoption.

At times Julie was suicidal, at other times she was self-harming, as she had been in the past. Once in the specialist unit she got into a rage and smashed two windows, so desperate was she to get out. These would have been particularly difficult times for Tina.

As well as self-harming Julie neglected to look after herself or care about her appearance. It was Tina who noticed that her heels were sellotaped to her shoes and went and bought her a pair to replace them – and later some toiletries.

On occasions Tina had to resist doing things for Julie which should have been done by professionals. The latter usually invited Tina to important meetings, consulted her and kept her informed. But it was the personal touch, the little acts of care, which they did not provide.

Throughout this time Julie was entering into relationships which seemed to Tina to be inopportune and inappropriate. Tina saw these as part of Julie's need to be loved.

Julie became pregnant and her boyfriend moved in to live with her. His presence altered the dynamics of Tina and Julie's relationship, as had the pregnancy. But Tina felt that despite these changes she had to continue to meet Julie. That was her priority while also seeking to get on with the boyfriend.

By now Tina became aware once more that Julie was not looking after herself: she was not eating enough. So Tina took her to the supermarket and bought food for her. As they reached the till she asked Julie if she needed anything else. Yes, she said, and went and collected a pile of chocolates and sweets: an indication, Tina thought, that Julie was needing comforters. After ensuring that Julie was well stocked with food, Tina taught her a bit about what constituted a balanced diet. Then Tina went and bought her clothes as well.

Salter, having read the above in draft, said that 'Tina had a very positive impact on how Julie felt about herself.'

Tina's story is typical of what each of the PROMISE mentors do for their young persons. In 2005 there were 130 mentors working with young people aged between 5 and 21 years. This was an increase of 40 on 2004 and was due both to an increase in volunteers and the inclusion of primary-age children in the scheme. And there are volunteers waiting to become mentors, once additional funding becomes available. The current mentors range in age from 24 to 73 years.

Tina's way of responding to Julie's needs demonstrated her readiness to go the second mile with her, a readiness Lyward also commended and demonstrated.

Tina made light of this involvement and its cost. Her motives, she said, included the wish to be the person for someone else who she herself had never had, and the desire 'to make something better for someone' (Harvey 2003). She was not alone among the mentors in wanting to put back something into their local community. When asked why they chose to become mentors, a frequent reply was: 'I've received so much and now here's a chance to give something back to others.' Other reasons given included wanting to enable a young person to make positive changes in his or her life especially when he or she might have been unable or unwilling to get help from others, to give the mentee the opportunity to be themselves without fear of judgement, to help him or her trust adults and so one day becoming a trusting and trustworthy adult for others, to provide a breathing space and some fun, to be a sounding board, if need be, to be someone the mentee could talk to who was not an authority figure and to offer a relationship where there was no agenda other than the chance for two people to get to know each other.

When asked, 'What difference have you made by being a mentor?' all seem clear that they have helped their mentee to make changes in their attitudes and lifestyles. Often this is described as 'we have become good friends'. In addition to this Tina and other mentors gave practical help. Perhaps what the young valued most was that their mentor was reliable, trustworthy and good company, turning up each week, keeping their word, giving an honest answer, having a laugh with them and being ready to chat about all sorts of things.

Learning with Lyward about unconditional love

This kind of giving of love and time to a young person, week in, week out, especially when he or she spurns the mentor or tests him or her out, becomes, before one sometimes knows it, unconditional. Sallie Roberts, who worked at Finchden in the late 1960s, realized she had to be available when needed. Any counting the cost or giving up by her could lead to the young person being let down. Such work is demanding and often heroic and not everyone is prepared to make the sacrifice it entails. But staying with and supporting the Julies, the emotionally damaged and insecure young people, works. It is what Lyward advocated to Sallie Roberts the night she got angry with two Finchden boys. She recalled it several years later.

People have said that nothing could be learnt from Mr. Lyward because he worked through intuition. I am not sure about whether intuition can be learnt but I am sure it can be awakened (it certainly can't be imitated), and that as time goes on one can come to trust it. But in any case, he taught other things more easily understood. One day I drove him to London to the retirement party of David Wills [a pioneer in the field of therapeutic community work with emotionally damaged youngsters]. He had undertaken to pick up two 15 year olds who had been spending a few days in London tripping on pills and had got exhausted and phoned to be taken home to Finchden. As we reached the party, he told me the place at Piccadilly where I would find them and told me to bring them to the party. I had been at Finchden only a few months and my job was supposed to be research [she was assisting Lyward with the writing of a book]! I hired a mini-cab and was lucky to have a sympathetic driver who held up the traffic in Jermyn Street while I persuaded the two that the mini-cab driver was not a policeman and that the Chief really was in town. Back at the party Mr. Lyward was having his photo taken with David Wills and A.S. Neill and was in no hurry to leave. My two friends stood at the door and offered obscenities to the guests as they left. After a while we started back on the 60 mile journey, through fog and with one of the boys screaming and trying to get out of the car as he came down from his 'high'. I made things worse by mistaking my way on the Maidstone by-pass and travelling several hundred yards on the wrong side of the dual-carriageway. When we got home the boy who had been so very upset and frightened offered to cook up a meal. We were all very hungry. After some two hours we faced a mess of tinned spuds, ravioli and baked beans. The other boy and I washed up and I began to reckon my chances of going to bed. Our cook then asked if he could spend the night in the Chief's side of the house because he didn't feel safe in his own room and he was told to make up a bed for himself in an attic room usually used for visitors. After some moments he came down to the kitchen, white and shaking, saying that the door of the room wouldn't open because a ghost was pulling it from the inside. Slightly unnerved myself, my temper broke and I told him 'not to be so silly', and opened the door for him. He went to sleep at once. Back in the kitchen Mr. Lyward showed every sign of entering into a discussion on the two boys. Still angry, I told him I thought they were a couple of hysterical little boys. He rounded on me and told me my views were too often facile. Then, more gently, he told me that if I wanted to work with disturbed and disturbing people I must be prepared to go on working 100% of the way (in his words 'to go with them twain') and not give up and lose patience when the job was almost done. (Roberts 1974, p.74)

Roberts concluded that Lyward's lesson was easy enough to understand but not to put into practice.

The PROMISE scheme, which is a county-wide Somerset initiative, has been evaluated and reported on by Penny Comley-Ross (2001). Rudi Dallos, a consultant at Plymouth University, enlisted her help when he interviewed six young people who had mentors and then held group discussions with mentors and staff (2005) from which the following quotes come. He sought to find out more about how young people experienced the scheme.

The mentees, three young women and three young men aged 13–17, willingly agreed that their mentors should know what they had said because they 'wanted them to know how much they had benefited' from their mentoring.

These themes emerged from the tape-recorded interviews:

1.   the mentor was seen as a 'good object'

2.   there was felt to be a good relationship which included

3.   a sense of attachment

4.   a mutual trust was present and

5.   the relationship enabled things in the mentee's life to change for the better.

There were positive descriptions of the mentor, such as 'she looks interesting…she is good' and 'she's really kind hearted' as well as accounts of how they had been helped. Within the good relationship were two strands: for some it was good because it was like a relationship with a parent and for others it was good because it was *not* like a relationship with a parent. For Annie there were both strands present.

She saw her mentor 'as a friend', as 'one person that has stood by me', but also sometimes 'like a mum', at other times 'like a big sister'. Their relationship stood the strain of a couple of arguments because 'there is so much of me in her and so much of her in me'. For Adrian what counted was that his mentor was someone he could talk to. 'I don't see my dad, and I didn't talk with my step-dad and I didn't really talk to my mum' (Dallos and Comley-Ross 2005).

There had developed within the six a strong sense of emotional attachment to their mentors together with a sense that they could rely on them especially when they were frightened, anxious or threatened in any way. Joan acknowledged the help she had had 'in sorting out things...if I am in a bad mood I phone my mentor and she comes and sees me'. Annie's mentor 'stopped me from slitting my wrists...she put me back on the rails' (Dallos and Comley-Ross 2005).

The resulting trust in the mentor and between mentor and mentee was built on several factors. The mentor's being available when needed was one. This included the mentor's readiness to put themselves out for their mentee and was confirmed by many mentors in conversation with the researchers when they said that they had to be willing to 'go the extra mile' for their charges. Mentors become someone the mentees can rely on both to turn up, and therefore not abandon them, but also to take their side, to stick up for them. Andrew recalled how he was taken to his mentor's house on their first meeting. This was something she was not supposed to do. But from the beginning she made him feel he was more important than rules.

He also described how he had changed from being very quiet to being able to talk to his mentor – about anything. 'I know I can trust her.' Thanks to her he was more able to trust others and form other good relationships. 'She has managed to make me trust other people.' Then the time came when the trust and the sharing became reciprocal. She talked to Andrew when she had 'a couple of problems' and he made suggestions about what she might do (Dallos and Comley-Ross 2005).

Some of the changes facilitated by the good relationship engendered included, for Luke, his being able to sit down and listen to his mentor when she was 'telling me what will happen if I get a criminal record... It didn't get up my nose...because I knew she was trying to help.'

In a good relationship we internalize bits of the other, through conversation with them, when we work with things they have said or suggestions they made, and through incorporating bits of him or her, such as mannerisms and gestures. Unconsciously we may even mimic these last two – together with the language and phrases the other uses.

From Dallos's research it is clear that the young people were able, thanks to their mentors, to move forward; to begin to put aside thoughts of their past as a dangerous time and to incorporate it into their present, and to contemplate a future which was hopeful. They were thus becoming better able to learn from and handle adversity and even take positive things out of it. Their self-esteem was rising rapidly. They were beginning to experience success, little advances, each of which was significant, a milestone reached. They had broken out of a cycle of expecting to fail.

Winnicott (1960) famously suggested that one could not be a perfect parent and that it was sufficient simply to be a 'good enough' one. The same appears to be true of mentoring. There cannot be a perfect mentor but that those aspiring to be 'good enough' will find in time that they have helped change their mentees' lives for the better and probably permanently. It is hard to think of a better justification for schemes like PROMISE to be funded well so that they can concentrate not on survival through fundraising but on assisting and supporting the young people.

Lyward's way at Finchden, of supporting and giving time and respite to the damaged boys who were referred to him, had much in common with the PROMISE way of mentoring. One Finchden advantage, one requirement Lyward insisted on, was that the contact was not once a week for two or three hours, but day in and out for months and years, and that it was offered by several staff and not confined to one adult. A second difference was that the boys themselves, 'the House', as Roberts said they were known (1974, p.72), were expected to play their part – to mentor each other.

The STAR charity: Promoting leisure interests

The PROMISE mentoring scheme gave birth in 1999 to the STAR charity, another Somerset initiative, devised by David Taylor of Social Services in conjunction with the Education Department. David Taylor enlisted the help of Rod Salter and Stella Marshall, after their success with the PROMISE mentoring scheme, to get it under way. They have been trustees and administrators of it ever since.

STAR stands for the Somerset Trust for the Arts and Recreation. It was created to enable youngsters in the county who are deemed to be at risk, fostered or in care, to have the opportunity to take up a hobby or pursue an interest of their choosing. Salter and others had noticed that this group had little in the way of hobbies or interests, had far less chance of pursuing them than other children and felt that there was little that was positive and successful about their lives. Furthermore, those who looked after them lacked the means and sometimes the motivation to encourage them to take up an activity.

A further significant factor, which I learnt from *God of Surprises* (Hughes 1988), was that we all have a creative side to us, something which we care passionately about and which is peculiar to us; yet if we do not use or express that side, we wither rather than flourish. That being the case, if we allow or encourage someone to pursue an interest or activity that excites them, then they could well become happier, get absorbed, surprise us and themselves, and add to the well-being of those alongside them.

From our schooldays do we not remember, and look back with satisfaction on, the things that we did which interested us rather than the school work we had to do or the exams that we passed? Does not the so-called extracurricular side of life stay with us long after the things we had to do have been forgotten? I am not suggesting that our qualifications did not matter at the time. Of course they did. Getting my O levels led to my taking of A levels, and so on. But now I remember the enjoyment of singing in the choir, of playing cricket and tennis, of walking to Avebury one non-school day, of being Second Citizen in *Julius Caesar*, rather than the essays I had to write or the notes I took for European history.

With these ideas incorporated into its philosophy, the STAR charity invites the young people it wants to help, through their carers, to 'Think of something you would like to do and get a sponsor. We will see if we can pay for it and link you with a teacher or club.' To become a sponsor one has to be an adult who knows the young person and be willing to send in a written request for funding. The trustees can then support the request, provided it falls within their remit and they have the necessary funds, and the young person can begin the activity.

A second factor in the thinking behind STAR is the development of resilience. Salter defined it as the 'capacity to do well despite painful and difficult experiences' (STAR Trust 2002, p.7). 'A resilient child is one who bounces back having endured adversity and continues to function well despite continued exposure to risk.' Such a person becomes more able to cope with school and to take up a spare-time activity. Salter suggests that those children who experience problems at home need to have 'havens of respite in other spheres of their lives'; they need to have a place to retreat to (which may not be easy to achieve) or something to do.

Lyward created Finchden as a haven of respite, somewhere where his young people could escape from their past external problems and in time find something to do which nourished their creative side.

I place more emphasis on the taking up of an activity as a way of developing resilience than Salter does. Surely the taking up of an activity can be the vital first step in breaking a too-familiar cycle of failure? Success at a chosen activity will rapidly build up some positive feelings about oneself as well as resilience, and both can then be channelled into school work or coping with family problems. The taking up of a hobby or activity might be the trigger which then brings about the breakthrough in self-esteem and expectations.

A popular scheme

This scheme, now in its sixth year, has proved to be popular with the client group and well respected and supported by those who have monies to back such enterprise. It has appealed to the general public's imagination as they can relate to a scheme which seeks to help some 500 children who are likely to have low self-esteem and usually get little encouragement and fewer opportunities to take up an interest or a sport. Somerset people and organizations have given generously to STAR. Some of the bigger trusts have also given substantial grants.

Who then benefits? So far over 320 children have received grants. In 2004, for example, the children elected, among many things, to learn the guitar, piano and flute; have singing lessons; go to karate classes; attend a weekly drama group and hire a recording studio so that a band could make a record. Some children attended a performing art summer school, some an activities week where four in one family sampled various sports including football and rugby. Several children had riding lessons and some went to football coaching – Yeovil Town football club was particularly good to two youngsters.

The choice is the young person's. The charity tries to make that wish become true.

Lyward saw to it that sufficient opportunities of this sort were available daily at Finchden for those who wanted to take part in them. There was no compulsion but everyone was encouraged to be creative and to use their particular talents and skills for their own benefit and for the good of the community. A good school will seek all this and more, as Freman College has demonstrated with its drama and many other opportunities.

STAR seeks to plug the gap in provision for the less fortunate children. Do those who get grants value such help? Most certainly. One child commented, 'When I'm riding I forget all my problems.' Another said 'Thanks to STAR I've now got my own saxophone. I never thought I would have one of my own.' A third said, 'I think every kid should know about STAR because it's helped me a lot.' STAR paid for a mountain bike for one youngster who reported, 'It keeps me out of trouble. I ride it all the time.'

I have a strong affection for STAR. This is partly because I was asked to become a trustee and then its chairman.

School Home Liaison Project

I learnt of the School Home Liaison Project through a chance meeting at a get-together to celebrate Dorothy Daldy's life. She had been a teacher and then a lecturer in psychology. She was also a churchgoer, (lay) reader and author. She had studied with Michael Ramsey and met Lyward at the Foundation conferences and had talked to me about him. Through Gay Drysdale, whom I met at that get-together, I learnt about the School Home Liaison Project which includes schools (mostly primary) in Camden, Islington, Westminster and the one primary school in the City of London, and works under the auspices of the London Diocesan Board for Schools.

The aims of the project, which has run since 1999, are to support each child in school, to encourage parents and carers to support and take an interest in their child's learning and to support teachers in their work in the school. Getting regular attendance has been one priority for some children. Another is to avoid exclusions. All the while high achievement is also being sought.

Three coordinators support school home liaison workers who are attached to schools in the project. Forty members were working in 48 places in 2001–2002. Additional funding is raised and their work is monitored and evaluated partly through their annual reports. The scheme is an example of good practice and an inspiration in terms of what can be achieved by imaginative voluntary partnerships. It is possible for such partnerships to cross local authority boundaries.

It would have met with Lyward's enthusiastic approval. For *Home and School*, which he edited from 1938 to 1953, sought to promote parent– teacher cooperation and to break down the barriers between school and home. It reported on the progress of Parent Teacher Associations which were just starting to be set up in the late 1930s. It published articles about children and young people, including one by Daldy (1938). It also published two collections of study papers, *Advances in Understanding the Child* (1935) and *Advances in Understanding the Adolescent* (1938b), which were both reprinted several times and to both of which Lyward contributed.

The project's emphasis on getting good school attendance from each child is crucial if schooling is going to benefit the child. This book and the conversations in it have largely concentrated on secondary schooling for two good reasons: Lyward worked largely with adolescents though he never lost sight of the fact that the child is father first to the adolescent and then to the adult and, second, that my experience and interest has been in a similar age range. But we all need to remember that good upbringing and the instilling of good habits begin with the newborn baby, and that everyone working with older children and adolescents is dependent and builds on what others have done before them.

As Brian Cresswell, musician and teacher, said at a recent STAR trustees meeting, 'The younger you start learning an instrument the more likely you are to succeed!'

Finchden: A one-off?

It can be argued that in one sense Finchden failed since it closed within a year of Lyward's death. It is indisputably true that it was remarkably successful. Burn's book raised such interest in Finchden that Lyward had to find time to answer the flood of requests to visit. No, it did not close because it had failed, but for other reasons.

The first reason was that Lyward failed to arrange for a successor. Prickett, who gave the address at his memorial service, had joined the staff with a view to his one day taking over from Lyward. But at some stage, by mutual agreement, both knew that would not happen. After that did he avoid choosing his heir? Was he – unconsciously – wanting Finchden to close after his death? Was he deliberately leaving things open and flexible so that the best possible choice could be made at the right time? I do not know the answers. But it was against his natural instinct to plan more than a short while ahead. It was as if his job was to deal with the present and to keep others in it also. Longer-term matters would become clearer in due course. His was a trusting approach, one which left the things of tomorrow until tomorrow. Such a lack of managerial grasp would not be approved in today's inspect and report culture.

His son, John, found himself in charge. He had been asked to work there by his father in the 1960s when his mother was ill. When his mother died he decided to stay on because his father needed him. On his father's death he assumed the leadership, more out of a sense of duty than from a desire to run the place.

Transitions are difficult times for institutions (e.g. Bettelheim 1950; Salzberger-Wittenberg et al. 1983; Stevens 1986) even if a new leader has been appointed. Anxieties abound and need addressing. John Lyward had to cope with them on top of an unusually tricky transition. And in addition there were further, major difficulties.

The financial position, often precarious, was now bad. Even before his father died John Lyward, as bursar, was faced with several thousand pounds' worth of bills to pay when there was £500 in his father's account. So he had to get an overdraft. Then there were the death duties on the estate. How were they to be paid?

Lyward had not been profligate with money. He had some expensive tastes but he ran Finchden not so much as a business but as a charitable institution. He never sought to make money. He was interested in helping boys to succeed. His fees were very reasonable and he reduced or waived them where necessary, if only to allow a boy to stay on. He did not take a salary, so he gave his services at something like cost price. The staff were paid what Lyward could afford to give them. No one made much money at Finchden, and the staff believed in the value of the work being done and in their capacity to contribute to it. In some way Lyward had touched and shaped their lives also.

Second, their architect, having looked at the building, reckoned that £50,000 needed to be spent on it more or less immediately. It had been loved but largely neglected. The fire prevention officer inspected the house and estimated that £30,000 would be the minimum necessary to bring it close to the requirements of the 1971 Fire Precautions Act.

John Lyward had no choice but to launch an appeal and a trust fund was set up. This did not bring in anything like enough money and so the decision was made, and announced in a letter (21 May 1974), to close the house, to find alternative provision for the remaining boys and to ask the staff to seek other employment. Finchden is now divided into five properties.

One member of staff who left at that time was David Hobbs. He recalled (1987) that after 30 years at Finchden he went away with £50. He received another £100 as a retirement gift from the trust fund.

Perpetuation in another form

Robert Brooks, who had drafted a book about Lyward, considered that Lyward had accepted that Finchden would close and that he had decided to perpetuate his work in another way (Brooks 1986). He would 'go out to those who would be the parents and teachers of the future'. He would do this by writing a book. As we know, this book never got further than typed drafts of the introduction, despite Sallie Roberts's efforts. (It could – with some skilful editing – still be published.)

It is part of my contention that Lyward was right to look to future parents and teachers to carry on his ideas. I hope I have shown (in Chapter 6) some ways in which that can be done.

I do not accept the claim that Lyward's ideas have had their time and are part of a bygone era. The bulk of what he advocated and did at Finchden is universal in application, works with children in any country and will not grow outdated. It will always be timely so long as there are young people to educate.

Besides, Lyward lives on!

Finchden may have closed in 1974 but its philosophy of care and the hospitality it embodied did not die. Lyward lives on in what he achieved, wrote and spoke about. He lives on in his former students and those who were at Finchden, in the teachers, social workers, parents, educationalists, administrators, psychiatrists, therapists and counsellors he inspired. His legacy is that no one need be thrown onto the scrapheap, no one need be written off. Ways can be found of reha-bilitating – he called it 're-educating' – the most difficult or damaged young person.

I hope too that he will live longer through this book. He was fond of telling the story of the missionaries who had been travelling in Africa. One morning they were surprised that their servants were not getting ready to set off. 'It's time to go,' said one of the missionaries. 'Master', came the reply, 'we have been travelling for two days and on the third day we rest in order to let our souls catch up!'

Lyward's legacy to us may include the reminder that we do well, from time to time, to let our souls catch up. Life is not a race unless we make it so.

We can let people develop at their own speed without hurrying them on simply because they have reached a particular age or stage. Hurry is not nourishing. It will not lead to true learning. Our hurrying a person on without taking into account his or her emotional and other sorts of readiness could be harmful, could delay his or her emotional growing. And if I feel impatient with someone, maybe it is my soul and not the other's that needs time to catch up! There is time, Lyward's life and work say to us – time enough.

'Half-Way Hopes'

To my fifth form English group
With acknowledgements to Philip Larkin's 'Born Yesterday'

I

A year ago you sat in your 'tightly folded' buds,
In pairs or alone, communicating
More by silence than by smile.
You trusted very cautiously.

To-day I see you very differently:
    Poised, becoming expectant.
There is a confidence and zip
About you that thrill me.
You have begun to 'gel',
    as they say
Not just as persons,
    for you were always that,
Though often you care not to
    give much of 'you' away;
No, I mean as a group,
    as Lyward and Priestley's inspector insisted,
As members one of another.

At this mid-G.C.S.E.-year point,
    may I wish you, Nicholas,
Stamina and forcefulness:
    you have the nicest of natures
Though still hidden.

For Sally joy – sheer unbounded
        fun and laughter
In waterfalls.

For all of you, especially the tempted,
Regular attendance.

Karen B. – to your energy and application
        add rhythm, a feeling for patterns
And old-fashioned attention to detail.

Pamela – you have so much to give,
        such presence: remember that gifts
Are for sharing. Silent conversation
        gets us nowhere, and a voice
Is for using: opera singers had to
        learn to talk first.

I am amazed by your recent progress, Darren.
You have a natural bubble inside you.
Put it to active use.
May you not run away from yourself.

You too, Jason, have taken off,
        once you decided you could do it.
You're the clearest advertisement
        for the educational value of golf!
Continue to talk about your dreams.

At times, only when we are riled
Do we dig for the concealed within ourselves.

By introducing you to *Macbeth* –
        (how quickly some of you took to it!
It was the first time any of you had asked
        to go away and read up what you had missed!) –
And Wilfred Owen's war poems,
        I was hoping that poetry
Would never be horribly hard again,
        though one of you wrote above
Born Again, 'Put ruddy translations'.

You have mastered the basics, Katherine,
    and you learn from life.
Banish 'I don't want to', and find
    encouragement in every lesson.

Jan, you can be a likeable intuitive fellow
    but I notice you keep justifying yourself.
Your determination to master a subject
    should be allowed its head.
I sense the beginnings of scholarship
    peeping through.

High hopes I have for you still,
    Claire, though months passed
When you seemed to have left the room.
You are getting organized now.
Preparation, of whatever sort, will pay
    dividends with your talking and writing.
Find your quiet centre first
    and work from stillness to activity.

Who can not like you, Karen C.
    even though I have not believed
Some of your excuses? You too should
    work from stillness
Rather than rush, reflecting
    first, writing later.

II

Catching you silent ones next,
    you have proved you can join in:
Isobel – in playreadings
    and discussion work.
Share your thoughts, bring yourself
    with laughter in from the cold.
Ride your suffering.

Daniel and Adam, you wanted to be known
    as a pair, but I've begun
To get to know you as individuals.

You're as capable, Daniel, as the next person
    of getting satisfaction from your studies.
Find the music in your voice. Like the lark
    or the eager singer, let it soar!

Adam – charm backed by appropriate action:
    we need to hear you
Burst in on a discussion, like a son
    dying to tell his parents his good news.

The enigmatic duo, Alan and Kin,
    you too hesitate too much.
Know 'he who hesitates is lost'
    can certainly apply to oral work.
Alan – your pen's tongue has been loosened,
    your own should follow.
May you discover the nourishing
    delights of conversation with any others.

Kin, steady and in the groove
    as a record player's needle,
Your courage and tenacity
    draw our admiration.
But to release the thoughts trapped
    within you, first make time
To read aloud the light and serious
    thoughts of others
In the privacy of your room until
    another's laughter no longer threatens.

Martin and Philip, carrot- and dark-haired,
    no one accuses you of silence
But at least some of your talk now goes
    outward, into our minds.
A rock on which we can all stand
    is your steadiness, Martin.
I've rarely heard you complain
    even though the going was word-befogged.
May you find in things near and far
    food for thought.

Between July and October, Philip
    your handwriting changed
And you found you could write essays.
    Learn now what a question
Is getting at, and keep
    questioning others.

Never – anyone – be satisfied
    with where you have got to.

Kathy, you've not known us long
    and you soon made friends.
Do not make the change of schools
    your excuse for marking time.
May you not be too easy on yourself!

Leon, you are incredibly neat
    And quietly meticulous,
Your silence is not stretching
    or shaping your mind.
So devour facts and rush
    to tell someone about them.
May you bubble with news!

No one can call you shy, Sarah,
    any longer. Take your reading
Seriously, devour words, defining them
    and letting them shape you.

III

To end with a more noisy trio
    who would not mind a tease.

Stephen, you have swung from a great
    reluctance to write anything
To bursts of creativity.
    Your enthusiasm is delightful
If a little overpowering. Channel
    it, swing true.

Ian's advance has likewise
    been most satisfying
Though he makes us less aware of it.
    May you plunder good books
And find a treasure above price.

Jon, how you've grown! A year
    ago you could hardly settle
Long enough to get your knees
    under a table. Decisiveness
Is what I wish for you, tied
    to a sense of direction.

You've none of you, probably,
    had to endure one poem
As long as this. May 1990
    find you all faring
Far better than you dared to expect.

JH, December 1989

References

Abbott, J. (1999) *The Child is Father of the Man: How Humans Learn and Why.* Letchworth: The 21st Century Learning Initiative.

Anon (1956) 'Healing and teaching.' Review of *Mr. Lyward's Answer.* In the *Times Educational Supplement*, 20 July.

Bausch, W. (2002) *Storytelling Imagination and Faith.* Mystic, Connecticut: Twenty-Third Publications.

Beadle, P. (2005) 'Fear and loving in the classroom.' *Education Guardian*, 12 July, 10.

Beeching, H. (ed.) (1936) *The English Poems of John Milton.* London: Oxford University Press.

Bennett, A. (2004) *The History Boys.* London: Faber and Faber.

Bettelheim, B. (1950) *Love is not Enough: The Treatment of Emotionally Disturbed Children.* New York: Collier Books.

Blandford, S. (2004) 'Master class.' *Education Guardian*, 28 September, 10.

Botton, A. de (1997) *How Proust can Change your Life.* London: Picador

Brooks, I. (ed.) (2003) *The Chambers Dictionary.* Edinburgh: Chambers Harrap Publishers Ltd.

Brooks, R. (1986) Personal communication, 7 April.

Burn, M. (1956) *Mr. Lyward's Answer: A Successful Experiment in Education.* London: Hamish Hamilton.

Burn, M. (1985) Letter to author, 5 November.

Burn, M. (2003) *Turn Towards the Sun.* Norwich: Michael Russell.

Cassidy, S. (2002) 'Edward de Bono philosopher lateral thinker in despair at the wasted state of British schools.' *The Independent*, 28 October, 11.

Claxton, G. (1998) *Hare Brain Tortoise Mind.* London: Fourth Estate.

Comley-Ross, P. (2001) PROMISE Year 3 Evaluation January to December 2000, an internal report sponsored by Groundwork, April.

Connolly, C. (1956) 'The Finchden experiment.' *Sunday Times*, 10 June.

Daily Telegraph (2004) 'The Dark Materials debate: life, God, the universe...', Wednesday, 17 March, 20–21.

Daldy, D. (1938) 'The limits of responsibility.' *Home and School*, 111.7, September, 131–2.

Dallos, R. and Comley-Ross, P. (2005) 'Young people's experience of mentoring', *Clinical Child Psychology and Psychiatry*, 10, 3, 369–383.

Dancy, J. (2005) Personal Communication, 20 July.

Danby, J. (1956) 'About Finchden Manor. 1. A poetical experiment.' *New Era in Home and School.* July–August, 167–8.

Dominion, J. (2003) 'The relationship between private and public immaturity.' *Audenshaw Paper 206*, June. Torquay: The Hinksey Network.

Earl, M. (1998) *Culture in a Bog: A celebration of 50 Years of The Theatre and Camping at Stratford 1948–1998*. Published privately.

Erikson, E.H. (1969) *Childhood and Society*. Harmondsworth, England and Ringwood, Victoria: Penguin Books Ltd, 239–266.

Freud, S. (1915) *Instincts and their Vicissitudes*. Standard Edition, 14, 109–117. London: Hogarth Press and the Institute of Psycho-Analysis, 1957.

Freud, S. (1923) *The Ego and the Id*. Standard Edition, 19, 3–63. London: Hogarth Press and the Institute of Psycho-Analysis.

Gardner, G. (2004) Personal email, 6 August, 1–4.

Gardner, W.H. (ed.) (1948) *Poems of Gerard Manley Hopkins*. London: Oxford University Press.

Gibson, R. (2002) Private memo.

Handy, C. and Aitken, R. (1986) *Understanding Schools as Organizations*. Harmondsworth: Penguin.

Hart, B. and Risley, T. (2003) *Meaningful Differences in the Everyday Experience of Young American Children*. Baltimore, Maryland: Brookes Publishing.

Harvey, J. (1991) 'A Study of George Lyward: His Ideas and their Application to Contemporary Education.' Unpublished Ph.D thesis, Exeter University.

Harvey, J. (2003) An interview with Tina Herbert.

Haydon, C. (2003) 'You there, see me after class.' *The Independent NQT Extra*, 20 November, III.

Hobbs, D. (1987) Personal communication, 15 April.

Horwood, W. (2004) *The Boy with No Shoes: A Memoir*. London: Headline Book Publishing.

Hughes, G. (1988) *God of Surprises*. London: Darton, Longman and Todd.

Hutchinson, F.E. (ed.) (1961) *The Poems of George Herbert*. London: Oxford University Press.

'Invicta' (1956) Anonymous review of *Mr. Lyward's Answer*. Kent Messenger, 8 June.

Keynes, G. (ed.) (1967) *Poetry and Prose of William Blake*. London: The Nonesuch Library.

Larkin, P. (1988) *Collected Poems*. London: The Marvell Press and Faber and Faber Limited.

Leeds University, Institute of Education (1957) Conference on 'Attitudes and Standards in Grammar School Teaching' Woolley Hall, Wakefield, 10–12 May, 573a–573s.

Lyward, G. (undated) 'Notes on teaching at Finchden Manor.' Unpublished.

Lyward, G. (ed.) (1935) *Advances in Understanding the Child*. London: Home and School Council of Great Britain.

Lyward, G. (1937a) 'Extracts from a diary, August, 1937' *Home and School*, August, 134–135.

Lyward, G. (1937b) 'Introducing the Committee of the Editorial Board.' *Home and School*, November, 186.

Lyward, G. (1937c) 'Extracts from a diary, November, 1937.' *Home and School*, December, 224–5.

Lyward, G. (1938a) 'Extracts from a diary, December, 1937' *Home and School* January, 256–257

Lyward, G. (1938b) *Advances in Understanding the Adolescent*. London: Home and School Council of Great Britain.

Lyward, G. (1938c) 'Feeling their way through.' *Home and School*, September, 115–117.

Lyward, G. (1942) 'A dialogue with myself (unfinished).' Unpublished.

Lyward, G. (1950) Editorial. *Home and School*, 15, 2 and 3, September, 26.

Lyward, G. (1953) 'A comment on standards: Particularly for parents' *The New Era in Home and School*, July–August, 119–122.

Lyward, G. (1958a) 'Unlabelled living', conference talk for *The Residential Care of Disturbed Children*. National Association for Mental Health, March, 5–11.

Lyward, G. (1958b) 'The child himself.' In Report on the Foundations Conference, 17 April. Unpublished.

Lyward, G. (1959) Lecture draft. 3 January. Unpublished.

Lyward, G. (1970) 'The school as a therapeutic community.' *Theoria to Theory*, IV, January, 17–32.

Mabey, R. (2005) *Nature Cure*. London: Chatto and Windus.

Marshall, B. (2003) 'Pupils need a carrot, not a stick, Mr. Clarke.' *The Independent Education*, 30 October, 3.

Mooney, A. (2004) 'Confessions of a private tutor.' *Education Guardian*, 24 August, 1–2.

Moore, C. (2002) 'A world without trust.' *The Spectator*, 7 December, 14–16.

Mullan, J. (2005) 'The Continuing Life of Tristram Shandy, Gentleman.' *Guardian*, 18 October, 10.

Niblett, R. (1957) Report on the Foundations Conference, April. Unpublished.

Niblett, R. (2001) *Life Education Discovery: A Memoir and Selected Essays*. Bristol: Pomegranate Books.

Nicolson, A. (2003) 'Russia's greatest tragedy in the making.' *Daily Telegraph*, 2 September, 20.

Nicolson, H. (1956) 'Learning to fit in.' *Observer*, 10 June.

Ninian, E. (2001) 'Value and meaning – the role of the emotions.' *Audenshaw Papers 194*, June. Torquay: The Hinksey Network.

Nixey, C. (2003) 'A day in the life of a new boy in school.' *The Independent NQT Extra*, 20 November, 11

Oakeshott, M. (1991) *Rationalism in Politics and Other Essays*. Indianapolis: Liberty Fund, Inc.

Oliver, H.J. (ed.) (1968) *The New Penguin Shakespeare: As You Like It*. Harmondsworth: Penguin.

O'Neill, O. (2002) *A Question of Trust*. Cambridge: Cambridge University Press.

Philibert, N. (2002) *Etre et Avoir*. BBC 4, 1 September 2005.

Prickett, J. (1959) Letter to his wife from Finchden Manor, 7 January.

Prickett, J. (1974) 'A memorial address.' *New Era*, 55, 3, April, 53–9.

Pullman, P. (2004) 'Opinion.' *Education Guardian*, 30 March, 5

Rilke, R.M. (1903) Letter to Frank Xaver Kappus, 16 July. Translated by Jennifer Cole.

Roberts, S. (1974) 'Glimpses into the community.' *New Era*, 55, 3, April, 72–4.

Robertson, S. (1963) *Rosegarden and Labyrinth: A Study in Art Education*. London: Routledge and Kegan Paul Ltd.

Robinson, T. (2003a) quoted in national 'One in Four' travelling exhibition seen at Somerset College of Arts and Technology, 19 September.

Robinson, T. (2003b) 'Judging from future experience...' *The Joint Newsletter of the ATC, the Charterhouse Group of TCs, and the P.E.T.T.*, 9, December, 46–7.

Rose, S. (2004) 'Education, education, education! Where have we heard these words before?' *Agora*, 3, August, 1.

Salter, R. (2005) Personal email, 5 July.

Salzberger-Wittenberg, I., Henry, G. and Osborne, E. (1983) *The Emotional Experience of Learning and Teaching*. London: Routledge and Kegan Paul.

Scott, R. (ed.) (1997) *No Man is an Island. A Selection from the Prose of John Donne*. London: The Folio Society.

Schwarz, C. *et al.* (eds) (1990) *Chambers English Disctionary*. Edinburgh: W.R. Chambers Ltd.

Smith, J. (2000) *The Learning Game*. London: Little, Brown and Company.

Spalding, F. (2001) 'A master of disturbing awareness.' The Wednesday Review, *Independent*, 15 August, 16.

St George's House (2003) 'The Future of our Schools: The Debate about Testing. Annual Review 2002–2003, 18.

Star Trust (2002) Somerset Trust for Arts and Recreation introductory leaflet, 1–7.

Stubbs, M. (2003) *Ahead of the Class*. London: John Murray.

Tanner, R. (1989) *What I Believe: Lectures and Other Writings*. Bath: Holburne Museum and Crafts Study Centre.

Taylor, R. (1946–1951) Personal file kept by G. Lyward, Finchden Manor.

The Times (1894) 14 January.

The Times (1973) 24 June.

Thorne, B. (2003) *Infinitely Beloved: The Challenge of Divine Intimacy*. London: Darton, Longman and Todd Ltd.

Tong, R. (ed.) (1996) Inspection Report, School No. 123863, 22 April.

Toplis, G. (1974) 'A royal course.' *New Era*, 55, 3, April, 63–7.

Toynbee, P. (2004) 'We can break the vice of the great unmentionable.' *Guardian*, 2 January, 22.

Ward, A. (2002) Editorial. *Therapeutic Communities*, 23, 1, 3–4.

Warren, M. (1974) *Crowded Canvas: Some Experiences of a Life-time*. London: Hodder and Stoughton.

Williams, R. (2003) *Silence and Honey Cakes: The Wisdom of the Desert*. Oxford: Lion Publishing plc.

Winnicott, D. (1960) The Theory of the Parent-Infant Relationship. *International Journal of Psychoanalysis*, 585–595.

Zeldin, T. (1998) *Conversation: How Talk can Change your Life*. London: The Harvill Press.

Further reading

Argyle, M. (1972) *The Psychology of Interpersonal Behaviour*. Harmondsworth: Penguin.

Ashton-Warner, S. (1980) *Teacher: The Testament of an Inspired Teacher*. London: Virago.

Astley, N. (ed.) (2002) *Staying Alive: Real Poems for Unreal Times*. Tarset: Bloodaxe Books Ltd.

Astley, N. (ed.) (2004) *Being Alive: The Sequel to Staying Alive*. Tarset: Bloodaxe Books Ltd.

Bridgeland, M. (1971) *Pioneer Work with Maladjusted Children*. London: Staples Press Ltd.

Dixon, D. and Cox, M. (2000) *The Disconnected Ape*. Axbridge: Interesting Place.

Gilbert, F. (2004) *I'm A Teacher, Get Me Out Of Here!* London: Short Books.

Gribble, D. (2004) *Lifelines*. London: Libertarian Education.

Holmes, G. (1977) *The Idiot Teacher*. Nottingham: Spokesman.

Lyward, G. (1938) 'Stay for an answer.' In G. Lyward (ed.) *Advances in Understanding the Adolescent*. London: Home and School Council of Great Britain.

Mackenzie, R.F. (1970) *State School*. Harmondsworth: Penguin.

Phinn, G. (1999) *The Other Side of the Dale*. Harmondsworth: Penguin.

Schumacher, E.F. (1974) *Small is Beautiful*. London: Sphere Books Ltd.

Shapiro, H. (1997) *Alexis Corner: The Biography*. London: Bloomsbury.

Skidelsky, R. (1969) *English Progressive Schools*. Harmondsworth: Penguin.

Thorne, B. (2002) *The Mystical Power of Person-Centred Therapy. Hope Beyond Despair*. London: Whurr Publishers Ltd.

Tolmacz, R. (2001) 'The secure-base function in a therapeutic community for adolescents.' *Therapeutic Communities*, 22, 2, 115–30.

Vallely, P. (2002) 'Modern education fails the spiritual test.' *Independent*, 9 October, 16

Walmsley, J. (1969) *Neil and Summerhill: A Man and His Work: A Pictorial Study*. Penguin Educational Special. Harmondsworth: Penguin.